# OPEN YOUR MIND
# TO RECEIVE

*Revised Edition*

# OPEN YOUR MIND TO RECEIVE

*Revised Edition*

## Catherine Ponder

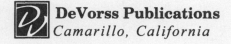
**DeVorss Publications**
*Camarillo, California*

ISBN: 978-0-87516-828-9
Fourth Printing, 2023

DeVorss & Company, Publisher
PO Box 1389
Camarillo CA 93011-1389
www.devorss.com

Printed in the United States of America

---

Library of Congress Cataloging-in-Publication Data

Ponder, Catherine.
 Open your mind to receive / Catherine Ponder. -- Rev. ed.
   p. cm.
 ISBN 978-0-87516-828-9
 1. Success. I. Title.
 BJ1611.2.P628 2008
 131--dc22

                                                2008008648

# Contents...

How she became unified with universal substance. Her mental acceptance brought results. The author's personal progress. The author's professional progress. An invitation to receive.

How a teacher prospered. How she made $30,000 her first year in business. Why a manufacturer failed. How a restaurateur identified with failure. How one man made a comeback from illness when he identified with good. How to identify with your source. The first kind of giving. The second kind of giving. The third kind of giving. The one who did not prepare to receive suffered lack. The one who prepared to receive prospered. How preparing for wealth attracted it. Prepare by speaking the word of receiving. Release is the final step.

The surprise power of release. Emotional scars are healed through release. Release works miracles in marriage. Release is a first step to success. Millionaire healed through release. The healing power of release. How letting go brought happy marriage. Release from others brought a new job and freedom. The written word of release brought freedom. Success for a schoolteacher who made a "forgiveness list." Letting go brought family freedom. Improve every phase of your life.

**Part I:** Prophecy through the spoken word. Prophecy through casual utterances. How casual words brought about a marriage. How casual words brought a gift of orchids. Prophecy through deliberate words. How Winston Churchill used words to win. How an independent trucker succeeded through words. How words healed her. How to prophesy with words. **Part II:** Prophecy through pictures. How an insurance company succeeds through picturing. How picturing brought $500. How picturing brought her "scrapbook husband." How happiness, contentment, and prosperity came to a businessman.

How a widow prospers. How a lawyer passed his bar exam. The results of a "first-class consciousness." How a realtor prospered. How to claim the best. The priests were millionaires. The Puritans stressed a belief in prosperity. How a schoolteacher obtained the best. How a doctor brought about remarkable healings. A nurse observes that attitudes determine recovery. How a new job and a new marriage came. Meditation upon the best brings the best.

The law of attraction. The widow who didn't want freedom from loneliness. Developing a "people consciousness" may bring changes. Why problem people are in our lives. How the author was freed from problem people. Speak the word of release. Release the people you love, too. Emotional freedom often leads to change. How to gain freedom from the opinions of others. How a doctor proved that the good of one is the good of all. What is right gives you a sense of peace. What you can do to be happy. How the author brought new people into her life. Brighten up your world.

The three phases of your growth. How a businessman successfully handled this second period. The prospering power of patience. Why a period of seasoning is necessary. How a young man lost his good. There are no straight lines in your growth. How to meet dark periods of initiation. When your life takes new directions, that's growth. What to do while awaiting the last phase of your growth. How to harvest your good.

The secret of prosperous increase. How he doubled his income in one year. How the secret of prosperous increase works. How America's early millionaires made it. How she paid off $15,000 indebtedness. An accountant's financial discovery. Why their income was $3,000 less. Prosperous thinking isn't enough. The public's fascination with this prosperity principle. Tithing gross or net. How a businessman caused his church to prosper. Where you give is important to your success. What about charity giving? Pray about your giving. Scattered tithes can bring scattered results. The prospering power of secrecy and release. A closing promise of vast benefits.

The author's discovery. The power of disagreement. The author's recent experience. From unhappiness to desired goals. A lesson learned. The power of biblical agreement. No impossible situation. From poverty to affluence. How immigrants succeeded. Declare it good. No experience is a failure. Agree with the good anyway. A decade of agreement works. Group agreement can clear out friction. How it works for those who are alone. Healing power. Agreement meditation.

# Introduction...

## IT'S TIME TO RECEIVE!

### An Invitation from the Author

With so much obvious financial need in the world today, why is a book about "receiving" necessary? Most of us might assume that to receive should be a normal process, especially in these economic times when almost everyone needs to receive on some level of life.

Yet a psychiatrist to the rich recently explained, "A surprising number of my talented, successful clients still feel unworthy. They feel guilty about having large sums of money. My job is to help them accept their good fortune and to enjoy it." For that service this therapist receives more than $100 an hour.

A famous actress recently said, "I used to think you had to be poor to be a genuine seeker of truth. Now I know that's just not so. You can be a seeker of truth while looking through the windows of your own jet plane, or while enjoying a luxurious hotel suite."

1

During an interview someone asked her, "How can you talk about spiritual values when you're surrounded by so much beauty?"

She replied, "Beauty and luxury are a part of God's kingdom so why not have the best? The important thing is that you do not sell your soul for such blessings. Instead, it is through spiritual growth that these blessings can best come to you and permanently remain with you."

## HOW SHE BECAME UNIFIED
## WITH UNIVERSAL ABUNDANCE

Religion has often equated healing with spirituality. We usually take it for granted that God as a loving Creator is interested in healing our sick bodies. If so, why wouldn't that same loving Creator be just as interested in healing our sick pocketbooks? God's blessings can operate in the field of finance just as surely as in that of health. Since God is the Source of our supply, true prosperity has a spiritual basis. Therefore, the financial phase of God's creation is as spiritual as any other. "The earth is the Lord's, and the fullness thereof," promised the Psalmist. (Psalms 24:1)

A businesswoman was once despondent over financial conditions. Her affairs continued to be out of order so she went out to the beach and sat there all day and most of the night. During that day on the beach she realized that the grains of sand are countless on the beaches of the world. That night she looked up and realized that the stars in the heavens are also beyond counting. She realized that the fish in the ocean lay so many eggs that if they all hatched, the waters would flood the lowlands. She thought of how leaves on trees continue to multiply year in and year out.

She became so aware of the abundance of the universe that she finally said, "YES! THE UNIVERSE IS LAVISH, ABUNDANT, EXTRAVAGANT, AND IT IS ALL MEANT FOR MY USE AND ENJOYMENT." As she began to feel unified with universal abundance, her thinking changed from limitation to bounty, and her affairs quickly responded, too.

Why should we go through life impoverished while living in a universe that is abundant in all things that are meant for us? As my series of books on "The Millionaires of the Bible"* has pointed out, the Holy Scriptures are crammed with such promises.

## HER MENTAL ACCEPTANCE BROUGHT RESULTS

A businesswoman recently wrote:

> I have found that if you obey the laws of prosperity, you will prosper—provided you learn how to *accept* that abundance. I have been busy experiencing my prosperity, and learning how to *accept* it. Here are some of the results that have occurred:
>
> In my line of work, raises are few and far between. Yet I received an unexpected sum, which had been negotiated for me. This was an added blessing. When I needed to buy two tires for my car, I was given the money to cover the cost! Money that has been owed me for a long time has started coming in. I asked for a rather reasonable sum one month. Instead, I was given *four* times that amount! A financial settlement of long standing is beginning to materialize. Relationships with people are changing fast for the better.

---

* *The Millionaires of Genesis*, rev. ed. 1987; *The Millionaire Moses*, 1977; *The Millionaire Joshua*, 1978; and *The Millionaire from Nazareth*, 1979; all published by DeVorss & Company, Camarillo, CA.

I have a huge lawn where I live. I didn't know what to do about getting it mowed regularly. I offered the owner the use of a large storage area I have. He graciously accepted. In turn he later offered to keep the yard up for me, and I graciously accepted.

Someone needed a picture of me. I said, "I don't have any, but I will see what I can do." Within a couple of weeks an employee who takes pictures for the people where I work offered to make a couple of nice pictures for me free of charge.

I needed more time so I decided to give of my time. I am reaping satisfying rewards. I was asked to help write a bulletin for our organization. Within a month I was appointed editor. Someone might ask, "What's so wonderful about that?" My answer: How better could I give of my time to an organization and at the same time receive training that can be priceless to me later?

I find that as soon as I receive any money I should sit down and write out my tithe check, then release it. This keeps the flowing going and growing.

Yes, I am working at this prosperity business. It is a whole new concept, so I have to persist at it. But with results like these (and there have been many more), it is worth the study and effort involved. This upward trend in my life is beautiful. And I accept its generous benefits, *all* of them.

## THE AUTHOR'S PERSONAL PROGRESS

I wrote my first book on this subject, *The Dynamic Laws of Prosperity*,[*] in the early 1960s while living in Birmingham, Alabama. It is known as "the magic city," and it proved to be so for me. I had begun developing my prosperity writings

---

[*] Catherine Ponder, *The Dynamic Laws of Prosperity* (Camarillo, CA: DeVorss & Co., rev. ed. 1985).

while living there in one room in the 1950s. My life expanded dramatically while I was in the midst of finishing that book. My expanded good included marriage and a move to the Southwest, where my husband taught at the University of Texas.

Much later, after my husband's untimely death, my life again changed. In the early 1970s, another move took me to the "Alamo City" of Texas. There I remarried and wrote the sequel to that earlier book while living for the first time in a home of my own, in San Antonio. This second book was entitled *Open Your Mind to Prosperity.*[*]

In the early 1980s, at a time when my life again underwent further expansion, it seemed an appropriate period in which to share with you, my readers, a sequel to the previous two books. That manuscript was written from my private studio, which was located adjacent to our home in a celebrity-filled neighborhood in the beautiful Palm Desert–Palm Springs area of Southern California. What a blessing to finally have the space and privacy I had so long needed for my writing, and an adequate staff to help with the many phases of my work. Still later, an update in the twenty-first century brought a move into more expanded living quarters in a quiet area of town. That move provided me with my own writing studio, a further accommodation to both my expanding life cycle and my working commitments.

As you can see, my own growth in opening my mind to receive has occurred gradually, over a period of time. I trust there is greater growth to come. Surely there are still prayers to be answered and dreams to come true. My mail has brought

---

[*] Catherine Ponder, *Open Your Mind to Prosperity* (Camarillo, CA: DeVorss & Co., rev. ed. 1983).

numerous reports of those who have experienced far greater good than have I. This convinces me that such expansion can happen to anyone who faithfully uses God's universal laws of abundance year in and year out on a sincere and consistent basis. The results will be in accord with one's own soul growth. The success philosophy I write about obviously does not contain a risky "get-rich-quick" formula. Instead, it describes a soul-satisfying process of growth that contains unlimited and eternal benefits into which one evolves.

## THE AUTHOR'S PROFESSIONAL PROGRESS

Opening my mind to receive has not only gradually brought more good into my personal life, but it has also opened doors in my professional life, doors I never dreamed would open.

After beginning to write on the subject, I conducted my first prosperity lectures in the Palm Beach area of Florida known as "the Gold Coast." Since that time I have been fortunate enough to be invited to lecture on the universal principles of prosperity in most of the major cities of America (and a lot of small ones, too): from Town Hall and the Waldorf Astoria Hotel in New York to the Phoenix Country Club in Arizona to the elegant Pioneer Theater Auditorium in Reno, Nevada. From Honolulu to New Orleans there have been interviews on television and radio, as well as numerous interviews by the print media.

The principles of abundance described in this book helped me to successfully serve one church in the Deep South and to found several others from scratch financially. My present global ministry reaches into all fifty states and numerous foreign countries. My books are now translated abroad and the lecture invitations flow in from all over the world. I regret that

I am no longer able to honor the many requests that are made, but I rejoice that I can continue researching and writing on the subject of abundance. The correspondence I receive from readers of my books around the world is filled with happy stories (some of which are recounted in this book) of how people in all walks of life have successfully opened their minds to receive. And they relate how you can, too!

Fringe benefits in both my personal and professional life have included listings in *Who's Who* and the *Social Register*, and the receipt of an honorary doctorate.

## AN INVITATION TO RECEIVE

A businessman in West Africa recently tried to cheer me on in my work by declaring, "More grease to your elbows!" May this book cheer you on and even add "grease to your elbows" as you proceed to study anew these universal laws of abundance. Even though you may have applied them before, as you do so now they can help you open your mind to receive greater good—greater wholeness—on every level of your life. And they can help you help others, too. (Remember, the word "prosper" in its root means "wholeness.")

Their application is especially apt in these economic times, when so many people are being forced to move from outer, material methods of acquiring prosperity to inner, mental and spiritual methods of acquiring prosperity. Prosperity should no longer be regarded so much as a matter of politics and economics, but more as a matter of increased understanding and growth. True abundance on all levels of life comes as a result of developing a prosperous consciousness. And "consciousness" is the result of ideas *held* in mind. So I invite you to take

the ideas found herein and *hold* them in mind. This process will
lead to appropriate outer action.

Then I invite you to write me about your subsequent experiences with abundance. It will be my pleasure to hear from
you as you join me in "opening your mind to receive"!

Catherine Ponder

PO Box 4640
Palm Springs CA 92263
USA

# OPEN YOUR MIND TO RECEIVE

— Chapter 1 —

Why should you deliberately open your mind to receive? Because most of us have endured a pinched, narrow existence for no good reason. We have blocked our good from getting through to us in the process. *There's nothing divine about a pinched existence. There's nothing divine about a narrow, limited way of life. It proves nothing but the foolishness and ignorance of human beings, who actually live in a universe of lavish abundance.* Those who lead a pinched, narrow existence are not expressing their true nature. They are only cheating themselves.

If this has happened to you, there is something you can do about it!

The word "receive" means "to accept." Psychologists tell us we can have anything we can mentally accept, but we must mentally accept it *first*. A great part of the act of receiving is thus to mentally *accept* the good we want rather than mentally fighting it.

9

A well-meaning young businessman who was obviously working on this kind of acceptance asked me at a book-autographing party, "Are all of those success stories in your books factual? Aren't *some* of them fabricated?"

"Why do you ask?" was my reply.

"Because they sound too good to be true."

"Just how long have you been reading about the power of prosperous thinking?" I inquired.

"Oh, only about a month," he said.

That explained his disbelief. He was still so conditioned to the limited beliefs of the world that he had not yet learned that "nothing is too good to be true."

I explained that for every success story that gets into my books, scores of others do not. The results of prosperous thinking are so numerous I cannot possibly relate them all. (And those reported to me are only a fraction of the happy experiences people have had who used the ideas suggested in my books.)

This young man was still trying to open his mind to receive. He was trying to mentally accept the belief that unlimited good is his heritage. To help him do so, I suggested he speak forth this well-known statement for at least five minutes a day: "NOTHING IS TOO GOOD TO BE TRUE. NOTHING IS TOO WONDERFUL TO HAPPEN. NOTHING IS TOO GOOD TO LAST."

## HOW A TEACHER PROSPERED

A teacher said, "Although I have studied the power of prosperous thinking for years and have had great improvement in my life from that philosophy, I recently discovered something I had been doing wrong. I had been saying I was on a 'fixed income.' And I had been trying to bring more financial income to me in a certain way. I had not opened my mind to the possibility of unlimited supply coming to me in unlimited ways.

"When I realized my mistake, I spoke these words aloud, over and over, for a long time: *'I am receiving. I am receiving now. I am receiving all the wealth that the universe has for me now.'*

"Within a few hours, I received a telephone call from the new cable television company in town, inviting me to come in and discuss the possibility of doing a number of children's shows for them on material I had already developed for handicapped children and slow learners. I went for the interview and this job is now assured. It is one that will bring me a considerable income.

"As I continued speaking the word of receiving, my retired husband's business quickly picked up. A number of customers appeared with furniture for him to repair. These jobs will keep him busy and happy for some time."

This woman continued daily to speak the word, to declare that she was receiving. Later she reported, "Money seems to be coming to me from all points of the universe. I have just sold a children's film which will be shown in schools as an entertainment feature for kindergarten and for underprivileged youngsters. Also, a film on games for children that I made months ago has now been marketed, and orders are beginning to flow in to the distributor. All this happened after I began daily to open my mind to receive."

*Many people fight their good rather than accepting it. They foolishly think they can neither have their good nor should they be asking for it.*

Those attitudes should be no part of the thinking of the child of a King. Do not burden yourself with such false ideas. Take just the opposite approach, as did that teacher, and see what happens as you open your mind to receive.

## HOW SHE MADE $30,000 PART-TIME
## HER FIRST YEAR IN BUSINESS

Most of us have heard a great deal about giving but not nearly enough about receiving. At the Christmas season, for instance, the emphasis is usually on giving, giving, giving. The result is that many people have a hang-up about receiving.

Giving is only one-half of the law of increase. Receiving is the other half. We can give and give, but we may unbalance the law unless we also expect to receive. Many people do unbalance the law by not expecting to receive—and so they do not.

As I wrote in my book *Open Your Mind to Prosperity*, a very beautiful and fashionably dressed woman once said to me, "When I first took up the study of prosperous thinking, I prospered so much so quickly that it startled me. I had just gotten a divorce and had only a few months' living expenses on hand. I decided to take a chance and use that money to go into business on a shoestring.

"I expected to make between $4,000 and $6,000 the first year from my new business. Instead I made between $4,000 and $6,000 during the first few months. I made $30,000 that first year in business, working part-time, and I will probably make at least $50,000 this year."

My reason for repeating this woman's story here is her final statement. She said, "My greatest problem has been in trying not to feel *guilty* about receiving so much."

*It is God's good pleasure to give you the Kingdom, and it should be your good pleasure to receive it.*

## WHY A MANUFACTURER FAILED

A recent newspaper story reported on a manufacturer of T-shirts who had gone bankrupt. The news story showed why: Thinking it a joke, he had placed this slogan on the back of each T-shirt: "Money isn't everything."

This man could not mentally accept the idea of prosperity in the form of money. He had not opened his mind to receive, so of course he did not.

You must be careful what you notice, talk about, or give your attention to, because that is what you are identifying with and that is what you will bring into your life.

Whatever you notice, you are inviting into your life.

Whatever you talk about, you are inviting into your life.

Whatever you identify with in your thoughts, words, and actions, you are inviting into your life.

If you notice, talk about, and identify with war, crime, disease, financial problems, or inharmony, this is what you are inviting into your own life. Through the law of mind action, it will come.

## HOW A RESTAURATEUR
## IDENTIFIED WITH FAILURE

There once was a man who thought he was about to go broke in the restaurant business. He invited me to eat in his restaurant. When I walked in, I could see one obvious reason why business was not good: His restaurant had such a dismal, uninviting atmosphere. I suggested he brighten it up if he wanted people to come there to relax and to eat.

On my way out, I discovered another reason why business was not good. Near the cash register was a "joke sign" that read, "This is a nonprofit business. We didn't plan for it to be. It just worked out that way."

The joke was on that man. He had mentally identified with "nonprofit" and that was what he had attracted. I suggested he throw away that sign and stop talking about lack if he wanted to prosper.

Identification with a certain state of mind will bring that state of mind and affairs to you, so be careful. What you notice, give your attention to, talk about, and get all worked up over emotionally is what you are inviting into your life—whether you mean to or not.

Open your mind to receive by noticing, giving attention to, and talking about what you *want* to bring into your life—nothing else.

## HOW ONE MAN MADE A COMEBACK FROM ILLNESS WHEN HE IDENTIFIED WITH GOOD

I once dined with a famous self-help teacher at his "hill house" overlooking Los Angeles. While on a lecture trip in that area, I had been surprised to receive his invitation to dinner because I knew he had undergone serious surgery just a few weeks earlier. Many who knew him were predicting that he was through and that he would be forced to retire because of his health.

Nevertheless, when I arrived at his beautiful home for dinner, he greeted me pleasantly. Other friends soon joined us and we had a happy evening together, as we chatted and reminisced about many things. His recent surgery was never mentioned. The state of his health was not discussed.

In spite of all the dire predictions, this man made a tremendous comeback in his health and in his career. He was soon accepted by an even more prestigious church than he then served. Next, he wrote several books on which he lectured during a round-the-world trip. (I had the pleasure of serving as one of the guest ministers in his thriving church while he was away.)

For a number of years thereafter he continued going strong. He spoke several times a week in his own church and elsewhere. He had a daily radio program, a dial-a-prayer ministry, and, on occasion, a television show. He wrote a book a year, as he had before his surgery. Only fifteen years later did he finally retire. When he passed on at the age of eighty-six, he had outlived most of his relatives, friends, and coworkers of long standing.

More than two decades earlier, when everyone said he was through, this man deliberately opened his mind to receive an inflow of health by identifying with the good. He made a comeback (when "they" said it couldn't be done) by concentrating on happy, pleasant things rather than by dwelling on the dreary operation he had just experienced.

## HOW TO IDENTIFY WITH YOUR SOURCE

Open your mind to receive by telling God what you want instead of constantly telling people.

Telling people what you want can dissipate your good, because God is the source of your supply—not people. Although people, ideas, and opportunities are all *channels* of your supply, God is the source because God creates those ideas and opportunities. Through the law of mind action, God helps attract the appropriate people and circumstances to you to expedite those ideas and opportunities through which your good can come to pass.

A statement you will want to use often to help you identify with the source of your good is this: "I DO NOT DEPEND UPON PERSONS OR CONDITIONS FOR MY GOOD. GOD IS THE SOURCE OF MY SUPPLY AND GOD PROVIDES AMAZING CHANNELS OF GOOD TO ME NOW."

## THE FIRST KIND OF GIVING

Giving is the first step in receiving. When you want to receive, give! However, there are three kinds of giving. All three are equally necessary to your long-term growth and success.

*First.* Give to God. Put God first financially. Why? As is explained in Buddhism and elsewhere, this is the first quality to be developed in your character on the road to enlightenment. Many conscientious people study self-help methods galore, yet do not receive the benefits from them they should because they ignore this first step.

*Various schemes have been suggested for getting rich quick. Most of them fail because they are based on "getting"— not "giving." They have no spiritual basis. The reason many people fail to receive their good in life is because they do not practice giving or returning impersonally to the universe on a systematic basis a portion of all that the universe shares with them.*

Two businessmen in Chicago once told me they had held the local franchise on one of the most famous success courses in America, one that cost thousands of dollars to take. Though they prospered for a time, they eventually went broke. They finally realized why: their course had only emphasized "getting"—not "giving." Their course had not taught the spiritual side of prosperity. It had not taught its students to tithe their way to prosperity by returning to the universe a tenth of all they received. Only after these two businessmen found their way into a local New Thought church and began to put God first financially did their financial affairs stabilize and they began to prosper permanently.

*When any persons withhold that which belongs to the universe, their lives are thrown out of balance, and they experience lack in some form. It may be lack of supply, lack of health, lack of love, lack of spiritual understanding, or lack of direction in life. Only as we let go of our littleness can we expand into the larger life.*

So it is not enough to say you believe God is the Source of your supply. You must *prove* you believe God is the Source of your supply by first sharing with God. This keeps you in touch with a universal source of abundance.

The billionaire Solomon pointed out what the wise use of this ancient success method could mean to you when he advised, "Honor Jehovah with thy substance, And with *the first-fruits* of *all* thine increase: So shall thy barns be filled with plenty, And thy vats shall overflow with new wine." (Proverbs 3:9-10, emphasis added)*

This success principle is more fully explained and documented in Chapter 7 as a method for helping you open your mind to receive.

---

* Bible passages quoted herein are from either the American Standard Version or the King James Version of the Holy Bible.

## THE SECOND KIND OF GIVING

*Second*. Give to yourself. Yes, open your mind to receive by giving to yourself, because *all progress begins with self-improvement*. It is sometimes easy to undergive to yourself, but that unbalances the action of the law and keeps your good from coming through. *You must first put your attention on the improvement and development of yourself, including your own strength and wisdom, before you can possibly help others.*

You cannot give to others unless you first have something to give. You must first have substance, along with a measure of strength and wisdom, before you can share these qualities with others. Some misguided people think it is selfish to emphasize self-improvement first. But *only after self-improvement are you capable of helping others.*

When you do the opposite, when you overgive to others, you feel depleted—and you *are*. It causes a sense of lack within you that is degrading and limiting. Because of this, overgiving to others is self-defeating to you and can be hurtful to those others as well. It accomplishes nothing constructive.

Psychologists talk about the sin of parents who overgive to their children. This suppresses their children's talents and overworks the parents. Such overgiving harms everyone concerned. In the recent "age of permissiveness," we witnessed the damaging results of overgiving parents in their confused, bewildered children.

By contrast, my own father gave as little as possible to his children, and what he did give, he gave reluctantly. The philosophy of undergiving had been a part of his upbringing. It caused many hardships for my brother, my sister, and me, and I needed years to overcome the poverty consciousness that resulted. So let us seek to strike a happy balance.

Shakespeare had one of his characters advise, "To thine own self be true." This might be revised to read, "To thine own self be generous." Give something to yourself right away. It might be a new book you wish to read, an item of clothing or jewelry, or something for your home or office. It might be the treat of going out to dinner, to the theater, to a party, or taking a vacation. It might be deliberately setting aside some daily time for prayer, meditation, and inspirational study. It might be something big or small, tangible or intangible.

## THE THIRD KIND OF GIVING

*Third.* After giving to God and to yourself, give something to someone else. After you give something to someone else, bless whatever you have given. Bless the person or persons to whom you gave it. Then release both the gift and the recipient. *Any of us—man, woman, or child—can transform our lives by transforming what we give—what we give to God, what we give to ourselves, and what we give to others.*

When you aren't sure what to give to others, that is the time to declare, "I GIVE UNDER DIVINE DIRECTION." Then watch the hunches and ideas that come. You'll be shown what to give, where, and to whom.

*Many of the blessings you want most are within your reach!* By your acts of giving, you open the way to attract the blessings you desire. *These blessings have probably been waiting to reach you but were blocked by your own lack of giving.* There was no free channel through which they could pass.

By giving under divine direction, you open a channel through which these blessings are freed to come to you. An early prosperity teacher of mine often said, "First give to God. Then give to humankind as God directs."

## THE ONE WHO DID NOT PREPARE TO RECEIVE
## SUFFERED LACK

After you give to God, yourself, and others, then get ready to receive! You can get ready to receive by preparing to receive.

There are those who say, "I give, but I do not expect to receive." And they do not.

An unhappy lady explained, "I teach a private prosperity class in my home, but I do not take an offering. I give, but I do not believe I should expect to receive." And she didn't, but she resented not receiving.

She *should* have resented not receiving, because she was unbalancing the action of the law of increase by giving, giving, giving, and not opening the way to receive.

It was pointed out to this woman that teaching such a class was fine, but that she was not only shortchanging herself, she was also shortchanging her students by giving them the impression they could get something for nothing.

She should have either charged handsomely for her course or opened the way right there in class for her students to prove the law of increase by extending an invitation to them to give generous tithes and offerings in appreciation for the priceless instruction they were receiving. She was cheating herself and she was cheating them by her fearful attitude.

## THE ONE WHO PREPARED TO RECEIVE PROSPERED

In the early days of the Unity movement, a visiting lecturer spoke to the workers employed by the Unity School of Christianity at their headquarters then located in Kansas City, Missouri. The guest speaker was introduced by Unity's cofounder, Charles Fillmore. Early in his talk, this well-meaning but somewhat self-righteous speaker said, "In my ministry, we do not pass the offering plate. We leave one at the back of the room and if anyone wishes to give something, the plate is available. But I do not stress giving."

According to the oft-repeated report, that's as far as he got! Charles Fillmore walked up to the lectern and said to the speaker, "You may think and teach what you wish in your organization, but in this one, we believe in passing the plate because we know the law of giving and receiving. Not only do we pass the plate in our meetings, but each plate is always filled to overflowing. Students of Practical Christianity want to give so they can prosper, and so they can help this movement to prosper."

It is little wonder that Mr. Fillmore later became known as one of the "pioneers of positive thinking" or that the Unity movement became a successful organization which has inspired millions over the years.

You can see how a contrast in attitudes brought a contrast in results. The woman who led the prosperity class did not believe in teaching the universal law of giving *and* receiving, and she did not receive. Her students were few. The other teacher did believe in teaching the universal law of giving and receiving, and he became the head of a prosperous organization that has helped countless people around the world.

*You can give up any false ideas you may have had about receiving. Your receiving doesn't stop anyone else's receiving. We live in a lavish universe, and there's plenty for all.*

## HOW PREPARING FOR WEALTH ATTRACTED IT

Several decades ago, the owner of a charm school was widowed and had three small children to support. People kept

saying, "She is a lovely girl, but nobody wants to marry someone with all those children. That's too much financial responsibility to assume."

This attractive widow paid no attention to that kind of talk.
She taught prosperity principles in her charm course. She told
her students they must develop a prosperous consciousness in
order to be charming and successful in every phase of their
lives.

She did everything that occurred to her personally to prepare to receive a better way of life. She bought a striking gold
designer's suit, which she constantly wore. It cost $200, which
was a huge sum for such an item back then. Once a week she
invited me to dine with her, always in the best restaurants,
though sometimes she barely had the price of our lunch.

Did the act of preparing for greater good attract it to her?
She married a widower of third-generation wealth, who helped
raise her three children, then later they had one of their own, a
total of four.

While everyone around her was talking lack and limitation,
she was quietly preparing for just the opposite, and what she
prepared for, she got! I find it interesting that none of the people who tried mentally to limit her future ever attracted wealth
to themselves—not through hard work, marriage, or a "wind-
fall." The limited thoughts they meant for her, they unwittingly
attached to themselves.

## PREPARE BY SPEAKING THE WORD OF RECEIVING

Many people's prayers are not answered because they keep
asking in prayer, but they do not follow through by getting
ready to receive.

Only when you have become ready to receive are you prepared for the next step: to speak the word of receiving (as, for example, the teacher earlier in this chapter did). When you daily declare that you are receiving, your words make a believer out of your subconscious mind, which then starts working with you to help make it so.

The way to avoid a pinched, narrow way of life is to deliberately speak the word of receiving. Declare daily: "I AM RECEIVING. I AM RECEIVING NOW. I AM RECEIVING ALL THE WEALTH THAT THE UNIVERSE HAS FOR ME NOW."

A businessman started doing this, and within one year his income became eight times what it had been.

Another businessman says he has received unexpected checks of $1,000 or more every time he has consistently declared: "ALL THAT IS MINE BY DIVINE RIGHT NOW COMES TO ME SPEEDILY, RICHLY, FREELY. I AM RECEIVING NOW."

## RELEASE IS THE FINAL STEP

As a teacher of practical mysticism recently said, "Students of prosperity need to know when to release the inner work they have done, then relax, so that outer results can come." There are resting places in mental action. "There is a time to fish and a time to dry your nets."

On various occasions in my life, greater good has come to me—after long periods of inner work—when I felt guided to release everything to its perfect results. I finished several books after I did this. Happy changes in location and business, a better income, and larger homes have all appeared after I worked inwardly, then turned it all loose, relaxed, and let go.

So after speaking the word of receiving for a period of time, declare that you *have* received, and release your concern.

Assume that greater good is already yours, since you have claimed it on the inner plane. This helps that good to appear on the outer plane as visible results—in rich, appropriate form under divine timing.

When you have reached this point of release, declare: "IT IS FINISHED. IT IS DONE. I GIVE THANKS THAT I HAVE RECEIVED AND THAT MY GOOD APPEARS IN RICH, APPROPRIATE FORM UNDER DIVINE TIMING."

As you then relax and let go, this process can open the way for unlimited results.

# YOUR GIFT OF RELEASE

## — Chapter 2 —

Now that you have opened your mind to receive in a general way, then relaxed and experienced greater good, you will want to get definite and open your mind to receive some *specific* good for yourself. There are many people who want and desire a specific good in their lives, but they do nothing in a practical way to *accept* those wants and desires—and acceptance includes release.

*You have many gifts you may not have used because you were unaware you had them.* One of your greatest gifts is that of release. The mystic Moses knew about this gift and asked his followers to use it for their prosperity in a certain way. Every seventh year was a "year of release." (Deuteronomy 15:9) This was a time when each creditor refrained from enforcing payment of that which was owed him. Every seventh year the Hebrews literally forgave all debts.

In spite of the Hebrews' having given generously in a multitude of ways, they were not impoverished by it, but prospered lavishly. They became a nation of millionaires.*

Your own gift of release is available on the mental, emotional, and physical planes of life. As you use it often, you will find that instead of impoverishing you, the act of release will enrich your life far beyond anything you could have conceived.

*The act of release is one of the most effective ways to open your mind to receive. The act of release frees you from tightness, tension, or grasping.* The act of release helps you to become an open, receptive channel through which the intelligence of the universe can flow to you to cleanse your life of worn-out relationships and conditions and make way for your new, expanded good.

The reason release is such a priceless gift is twofold: *First,* it eliminates negativity from your life. *Second,* it expands your good. *Elimination of something from your life is always an indication that something better is on the way. Elimination not only takes something from you, but it also gives something to you.*

So you need never be fearful of letting go. That which still belongs to you is never lost through the act of release. Instead, your expanded good is much freer to move into your life.

People sometimes say, "I am afraid of the word 'release.' How do I know my subconscious mind will release the right thing?"

You can be confident that the right thing will happen because your subconscious has a way of releasing that which has bothered you most, whether you were consciously aware of it or not. The act of release also calls into action your supercon-

---

* See *The Millionaires of Genesis, The Millionaire Moses,* and *The Millionaire Joshua.*

scious or Christ Mind, which is filled with universal intelligence. It always knows what to release. There is no danger in speaking the word of release when you ask the Christ Mind within you to do the releasing in your life.

## THE SURPRISE POWER OF RELEASE

Some interesting things once happened to me during a period when I was using this statement daily: "CHRIST IN ME NOW FREES ME FROM ALL RESENTMENT OR ATTACHMENT TOWARD OR FROM PEOPLE, PLACES, OR THINGS OF THE PAST OR PRESENT. I MANIFEST MY TRUE PLACE WITH THE TRUE PEOPLE AND WITH THE TRUE PROSPERITY NOW."

I had been living in an apartment that was not of my choosing. It was selected by my then teenage son and it suited his needs perfectly, but I never cared for it. After he enlisted in the military in the mid-1960s, I was left living in "his apartment," with extra bedrooms and baths I no longer needed. There were also household effects and furniture I wished to release because of personal memories attached to them.

After he left, I often thought, "I must get busy and find an apartment I like. There's no reason for me to remain in this one any longer." But I never got around to doing so. A year later I was still living in "his apartment."

Within two weeks of the time I started declaring that Christ in me was freeing me from attachments toward or from people, places, or things of the past or present, I received a telephone call from a friend saying that space would soon be available in an apartment complex I had long admired. Moving into that apartment would mean getting rid of my unwanted furniture and household effects, because it was smaller and more compact.

The manager there was a reader of my books, wanted me as a tenant, and even promised to redecorate the entire apartment if I would take it. Soon I was installed in my hilltop apartment with a lovely view of the city. I was surrounded by beautiful new furnishings and free from memory-filled ones of the past. I marveled at the words of release that had freed me from unwanted conditions and possessions.

As I continued declaring freedom from attachment toward or from people, places, or things of the past or present, some people in my life let me go. I had felt for months that our relationships had run their course, but had not known how to sever them graciously. When I spoke words of release, those people found other interests and simply faded out of my life.

As I continued speaking words of release, the next thing that happened was a surprise: I received a long-distance call from a childhood friend whom I had not seen in fifteen years. She felt mistakes had been made in an incident that occurred between us twenty-five years previously, and she was still condemning herself for the way things had worked out between us. (I had forgotten the incident.) I had no way of knowing of her feelings until she responded through the ethers to my words of release and then telephoned me. In that conversation I put her mind at ease by speaking words of release to her about the incident of twenty-five years' standing.

*So often we try to force new good into our lives when we have not yet made room to receive it. Release helps us to turn loose the old to make way for the new.*

## EMOTIONAL SCARS ARE HEALED
## THROUGH RELEASE

Some people assume that all they need to do is speak the word of release a few times in order to get freedom from bondage. Since the subconscious feeling nature of human beings is packed with unhappy memories and negative emotions, we must speak the word of release often and deliberately to gain freedom from unhappiness and limiting experiences of the past. Like the Hebrews, we all need to practice the art of release—continuously.

A woman in her eighties was having financial difficulties. Through talking with a friend she realized that she needed to release unhappy experiences of the past, so as to make way for increased prosperity in her life.

At the age of twenty, she had become engaged but her father broke up the romance and she never married. Sixty years later she sat and cried about this broken romance and the unhappy life she felt had followed. She blamed all her misery on her father. Both her father and her former fiancé had long since passed on, yet she continued holding onto this unhappiness over a sixty-year period.

The statement that helped this woman was the one already mentioned: "CHRIST IN ME NOW FREES ME FROM ALL RESENTMENT OR ATTACHMENT TOWARD OR FROM PEOPLE, PLACES, OR THINGS OF THE PAST OR PRESENT. I MANIFEST MY TRUE PLACE WITH THE TRUE PEOPLE AND WITH THE TRUE PROSPERITY NOW."

## RELEASE WORKS MIRACLES IN MARRIAGE

Release can work miracles in marriage, too. One wife said, "For nearly twenty years I struggled to make a go of my marriage, with little success. There were strain, strife, trial separations, and all kinds of trouble between us. I have now found the key to successfully living with my husband: release him, forgive him, loose him. Also, an inharmonious work situation has become friendly and comfortable through releasing and forgiving. Release is the answer to everything!"

## RELEASE IS A FIRST STEP TO SUCCESS

Once on a lecture trip in Canada, I met a businessman who conducted success seminars all over that country. He said he had discovered that release is one of the first steps to success and that he emphasized the release principle in his teaching. Later he wrote me how release had worked for him:

Personally, for me to gain an understanding of the release principle changed my life. It removed what I had felt was an impossible problem. *Many of my business and personal problems have been corrected through meditation periods in which I dwelled upon "release."*

Another businessman said:

For nearly five years I had been praying about certain circumstances in my life and using various affirmations. The circumstances did not clear up until I learned the wonderful power there is in the word "release."

Since I have practiced release over the past three or four years, amazing results have come in my contracting business. Once when a crew of my employees tried to get a large compressor started, the engine would not catch. They tried repeatedly for over an hour before calling me. I tried to locate a mechanic, but none would be available for hours.

So I prayed, "Lord, You can get that compressor started if You want to. This is Your business. Do what You will in this situation. I release the matter to You." Later that day the workmen came in looking puzzled. One of them said, "It was the strangest thing. We had worked over that engine for at least an hour, and it just wouldn't start. After talking with you, I decided to try one more time to start the compressor. When I put my finger on the starter button, the engine roared to life."

This man concluded, *"Release is a word that works miracles."*

## MILLIONAIRE HEALED THROUGH RELEASE

Release is the topside of forgiveness. The word "forgive" means "to give up," as in giving up a resentment or a claim. When you speak words of release, you start the action of forgiveness, or giving up. If there are people or situations in your life you have tried to forgive but were not able to because of antagonisms and negative feelings that got stirred up in the process, then stop trying to forgive them. Just release them. As you loose them and let them go through release, you are forgiving them by giving them up.

A retired millionaire once sat in a wheelchair in his lovely mansion. Surrounded by servants, he was brooding over bitter experiences of the past. Along with several other health problems, he was suffering from a blood clot in his foot, which physicians had said would keep him from ever walking again.

Upon learning of the healing power of release, this man began to declare: "CHRIST IN ME NOW FREES ME FROM ALL RESENTMENT OR ATTACHMENT TOWARD OR FROM PEOPLE, PLACES, OR THINGS OF THE PAST OR PRESENT. I MANIFEST PERFECT HEALTH NOW."

Within ten days the blood clot had cleared up, he was walking again, and his doctor was mystified. His health steadily improved as he continued clearing out bitterness and resentment from both his mind and his body through daily words of release.

## THE HEALING POWER OF RELEASE

Release has healing power for such ordinary problems as headaches, too. A woman had spent the winter in Florida and returned north earlier than expected. When she arrived home, she found that her caretaker had not properly followed her instructions. The furnace was not working and snow was piled up in front of her house.

Seeing the situation gave her a terrific headache. When medication did not relieve it, she began to say to herself: "RELEASE, LOOSE, LET GO, LET GOD." To the caretaker she mentally said: "I FULLY AND FREELY FORGIVE YOU. I LOOSE YOU AND LET YOU GO. I LET GO AND LET GOD."

Her headache disappeared within an hour, after which she literally released her caretaker by firing him. Sometimes the best way to "forgive people" is to "give *them* up."

## HOW LETTING GO BROUGHT HAPPY MARRIAGE

A woman had been through the bitterness of divorce, not just once but several times. At a very low moment in her life, she learned about the wisdom of release and began releasing unneeded clothes and household effects. Later she released a house she no longer wanted. She sold it and moved into an apartment that seemed right for her.

She even released old love letters she had clung to for years, letters connected with a former marriage. After releasing much and moving into the apartment, she was led to a fine new job. Later she met a businessman whom she happily married. She explained her new life in this way: *If one can really let go, all kinds of good things happen.*

## RELEASE FROM OTHERS BROUGHT
## A NEW JOB AND FREEDOM

After twenty-five years of marriage, a woman went through a divorce she did not want. Two friends helped her through that difficult period.

Later she realized she had become overly dependent upon her friends emotionally and needed to take responsibility for her own well-being. She was wondering what she should do— when she heard about release. She began to declare every day: "I LET GO OF EVERYTHING AND EVERYBODY THAT IS NO LONGER A PART OF THE DIVINE PLAN OF MY LIFE. I NOW EXPAND QUICKLY INTO THE DIVINE PLAN OF MY LIFE, WHERE ALL CONDITIONS ARE PERMANENTLY PERFECT."

Her release came in a strange way (as it often does). Along with these two women, she was a member of a club in which she had served as treasurer for some time. After she began declaring words of release, the club members decided to have the books audited. Soon after this woman turned the books over to another member for auditing, the auditor claimed there was a $600 deficit. Although the claim later proved to be false, the woman said the accusation was worth it because she never heard from the other two women again! "If they don't find their error, I'll pay it as an act of charity," she quipped.

As she continued dwelling on release, she obtained a good job as the manager of a bookkeeping firm. She said, "I feel freer than I have in years. I can do anything I want without wondering what 'they' will think. I am glad to be out of a rut at last."

## THE WRITTEN WORD OF RELEASE
## BROUGHT FREEDOM

Along with speaking words of release, it is also good to write out that which you wish to eliminate from your experience. During one period in my life I had a nagging problem that overshadowed everything else. For years I tried to get free of it. I pictured freedom and affirmed it, but the problem hung on. Then I hit upon the idea of making an "elimination list" at the first of the year, on which I wrote down my desire to be free from that challenge. That year the problem was finally eliminated from my life, which convinced me that writing down what you want eliminated from your life can be a powerful form of release.

## SUCCESS FOR A SCHOOLTEACHER
## WHO MADE A "FORGIVENESS LIST"

A schoolteacher learned of the magic power of release and decided to try the written method. She said:

> I read about a woman who put aside a certain time every day to forgive others who had mistreated her. Through that method, all wrongs were rectified.
>
> I realized that I, too, harbored much resentment from apparent mistreatment, and that my resentment was blocking the way to my good. I took a sheet of paper. On one side I listed everyone against whom I felt resentment. On the other side, I listed the good I wanted to come into my life.
>
> Every evening I had a meditation period in which I blessed and forgave all whom I had resented. Then I turned my paper over and gave thanks for my increased good. My list of desires included a new car, driving lessons, good classes to teach in school, and interesting lessons. (Last year

my classes were composed of children who had some of the worst disciplinary problems in the whole school.)

As I persisted in going over my list every day, the good began to pour in. In the face of many obstacles, I obtained my car. I have had such good classes in school this year that all the teachers say it must be a mistake. I have had not one problem child this semester. Also I have been blessed with going abroad, doing graduate study, and traveling extensively in this country.

## LETTING GO BRINGS FAMILY FREEDOM

A widow had often heard the phrase "let go and let God." She assumed it meant giving up on the problem rather than getting free from it.

Then she found these words, which fascinated her: "I FULLY AND FREELY FORGIVE. I LOOSE AND LET GO. I LET GO AND LET GOD. CHRIST IN ME IS MY FORGIVING POWER. CHRIST IN ME IS MY RELEASING POWER. CHRIST IN THIS SITUATION IS ITS FORGIVING POWER NOW, AND ALL IS WELL."

As she declared these words, fear and grief left her. She realized that to "let go and let God" meant just that: to give up the hurt—to let God absorb it into Infinite Love.

It was a relief for her to learn that there was neither repression nor hurt feelings in forgiveness. There was no strain, only freedom and peace. She said:

I had always worshipped my daughter. I had shielded her from every problem and been careful to see that nothing ever hurt her. I began to see that during the years she and her husband lived in an apartment near me, I was under severe strain. I was so dependent on their love that I was in constant fear of their slightest disapproval. They knew this and took outrageous advantage of me. They used the threat of withdrawing their love to hold me in line. I am now free, because I realize that God is the Source of my good, not my family. Loosing and letting go has brought me peace of mind and freedom.

## IMPROVE EVERY PHASE OF YOUR LIFE

You can improve all levels of your life through accepting your gift of release. Elimination of the old makes way for your increased, expanded good. An eighty-year-old man had been unable to find work. He learned of the magic power of release and decided to release a house filled with furniture he no longer wanted. He said, "After I cleaned out the first closet, I got a job immediately."

A secretary heard of the magic power of release and quit her job that same day. It seemed a foolish thing to do because her boss had just given her a raise and she needed the money. Nevertheless, she quickly went into the freelance art business, learning as she worked. She soon was selling hundreds of story and cover illustrations for children's magazines. Later she wrote stories and articles and even had a handicraft book published. But none of this success came until she released a job she no longer wanted.

*Remember, the elimination of something from your life is always an indication that something better is on the way!*

A woman decided to invoke her gift of release by resigning from a fine government job she had held for ten years. She wanted to remain at home with her children. Her husband heartily approved. The magic of release did its perfect work. Her husband's income in his sales work doubled during the next year and they never missed her income. Release had brought prosperity and freedom.

Remember: You never lose anything that is still for your highest good through the act of release. Instead you make way for your expanded good to come to you.

A lawyer had grown restless with his practice. He was not doing what he really wanted to do. He decided to invoke the magic power of release by giving a month's work to a young attorney who had just opened a law office nearby. The same day the first attorney did this, a new client walked into his office and hired him as a corporation lawyer, which is what he had wanted to be. His income soon doubled—thanks to release.

Accept your gift of release and use it often. It will open up a happier world to you!

# YOUR GIFT OF PROPHECY

## — Chapter 3 —

You may have thought of the "gift of prophecy" as a special spiritual or psychic gift bestowed upon only a few, such as the prophets of the Bible, who used their gift of prophecy with amazing results. Yet you have this gift of prophecy too, which you can use in simple ways to help you open your mind to receive increased good in every phase of your life.

What is your gift of prophecy? How can you put it to work?

## PART I:
## PROPHECY THROUGH THE SPOKEN WORD

The word "prophecy" means "a declaration of something to come." It also means "a prediction of the future under divine guidance" or simply "an intuitive prediction." You are constantly using your gift of prophecy through the predictions, declarations, words, and decrees that you speak forth about yourself and others. Your spoken words are your gift of prophecy.

*If you are not satisfied with your life, you can begin using your gift of prophecy to improve it. As you change your words, you change your world. As you improve your words, you improve your world. As you transform your words, you transform your world.*

You can invoke your gift of prophecy through the use of your words in two ways. *First*, through your casual utterances, your everyday words. *Second*, through your deliberate words and predictions, such as verbal affirmations.

## PROPHECY THROUGH CASUAL UTTERANCES

Your casual words are very powerful, because you generally speak them forth in a relaxed state of mind, in which there is no mental block to their manifestation. Therefore, those words often produce results for you quickly.

In the mid-1960s, I watched my casual words produce some startling results. I was moving out of that apartment my son and I occupied before he went into the military. Even though I employed a professional to make the actual move, I felt I needed extra help getting ready for it.

This was the first time in years my son had not been with me in the midst of a move. I missed having his help. I found myself thinking, "If only Richard were here, this move would be so much easier. He would know what to do about many things."

Then I reminded myself that I must release him to his new life. Nevertheless, I often still found myself thinking, "If only Richard were here."

One day in the midst of my moving preparations, some neighborhood children appeared and asked if they could help me. It was a hot summer day and they were restless and bored with their usual activities. After receiving permission from their parents, I put them to work.

Everything went well for several hours, and I was saying to myself, "My decree has worked, even though someone else's children have appeared to help me prepare for this move."

Then there was a knock at the door. When I answered it, I saw a tall young man (about the height of my son) standing there. He said, "I understand you are moving. My little brothers and sisters are already here helping you, and I came to help, also."

With delight I replied, "Fine, and what is your name?"

"My name is Richard."

My gift of prophecy had worked. I had been saying for days, "If only Richard were here," and suddenly a "Richard" appeared. He did all the things my son would have done.

Sometimes our casual words do not manifest results so quickly, but such decrees—persistently spoken—*do* manifest results for us in due time.

## HOW CASUAL WORDS
## BROUGHT ABOUT A MARRIAGE

As a child, I often visited the home of an "old maid" aunt, who provided a place to live for her elderly parents and several unmarried brothers and sisters.

Whenever this maiden aunt got provoked with members of the family, she always made the same threat: "One of these days I am going to Florida and getting married." Her words became a standing joke in the family. Her "prophecy" seemed incredible, even impossible, and nobody paid any attention to it.

As the years passed, her brothers and sisters married and moved out of the family home. Finally, both of her parents passed on within a short time of each other, and she sold the family home—and went to Florida to live and to work.

By this time she was in her late forties. A year later my family received a postcard from her that read: "Last week Mr. Brown and I were married in Gainesville."

You can imagine the reaction in her family back home. Nobody had ever heard of "Mr. Brown," though they discovered he was a very nice widower whom she had met in connection with her work. Now, after many years of marriage, they are still busy "living happily ever after."

Your words are your gift of prophecy. Sometimes your most casual words, repeatedly spoken, are your greatest gift of prophecy. That aunt proved it.

## HOW CASUAL WORDS
## BROUGHT A GIFT OF ORCHIDS

*One of the greatest ways you can help other people is to speak forth casual words predicting good on their behalf. Often you can mentally accept good for others that they have not yet been able to mentally accept for themselves.*

Once when I lectured at a convention, a friend gave me a beautiful orchid to wear. The convention was to continue for several days after I had spoken. A special friend of mine was also there, scheduled to speak a couple of days after I left.

Since the orchid would still be fresh at the time she spoke, I thought, "I must give my friend this orchid to wear." But in the rush of activities, I never got the orchid to her, even though I had given it to her mentally.

Later in correspondence between us I said to her, "I mentally gave you my orchid although I never got it to you in person. I prophesied an orchid for you, so someone else will give you an orchid very soon."

She wrote back, "It's a beautiful idea but nobody ever gives me orchids."

About two months later I received a happy letter from her in which she said, "You can prophesy for me any time you want to! I have been given *four* orchids since you decreed it. Relatives and friends have given me orchids on every special occasion since then—my birthday, Easter, etc."

## PROPHECY THROUGH DELIBERATE WORDS

Deliberate affirmations, formally spoken forth, are the second way of using your gift of prophecy.

In this age of enlightenment that is now dawning, *any person who does not know the power of the word is behind the times.*

Large numbers of people are reading the countless self-help books that are now on the market. Yet many of those readers are not getting the practical results they expect. Often they complain that self-help theories do not work for them.

*Most people who read self-help books have learned enough to change the course of their lives, if only they would use what they have learned.* One way for them to do that is to use their gift of prophecy. A single bold statement declaring how you want your life to be is worth more than dozens of books read or lectures attended. Spoken words describing the good you want will help you claim it and quickly release it into your own life. "Ye have not, because ye ask not." (James 4:2 ASV)

## HOW WINSTON CHURCHILL USED WORDS TO WIN

One of the well-known stories concerning British Prime Minister Winston Churchill is about how he turned the tide of the war during the Battle of Britain in World War II. Everyone in England was prophesying defeat. Many felt they had already lost the war.

Mr. Churchill went on radio and declared, "We shall win by land. We shall win by sea. We shall win." He talked like a winner and, in the opinion of many historians, his words were the turning point in the war.

## HOW AN INDEPENDENT TRUCKER
## SUCCEEDED THROUGH WORDS

Many years ago, when I heard about an independent trucker who was very successful, I began to think about how our words can create conditions. Even when business was hard to find, his two trucks were always on the road working.

When someone asked the secret of his success, he spoke of the time when he had hit rock bottom financially. He could not find business, the payments on his truck were overdue, and he had no cash. Sitting in a lonely hotel far from home, he opened his Bible to the thirty-seventh chapter of Ezekiel. There he read of the prophet's vision about the dry bones—when Jehovah told Ezekiel to prophesy to those dry bones, and when he did, the dry bones rose up and came to life as people.

The trucker decided there was a powerful success formula in that old Bible story. He went out to his truck, placed his hand on its dusty fender, and prophesied, "Listen, I prophesy that you will be working again tomorrow. What's more, it will be a good-paying load." He immediately felt better, went back to his hotel, and retired for the night.

At five o'clock the next morning, his telephone rang and a voice said, "I have a load of butter that's got to get to Los Angeles in a hurry. Can you take it?"

Of course he could—and he did.

In commenting later on the power of prophesying success, this man said, "I have been in tight places since then but I always knew I could get out. I have prophesied that a soft load would not spoil until I could get ice, and it came through all right. I have prophesied that a bad road over which I was driving my truck would get better, and it did. I even prophesied that I would have a second truck some day, and now I have."

You can use your simple but powerful gift of prophecy through your spoken words to produce great good in your own life and in the lives of others.

## HOW WORDS HEALED HER

A young woman from Kentucky moved to Colorado with her family because one of her parents was suffering from a disease the Colorado climate was supposed to help.

After moving, she began attending an inspirational class that met in a friend's parlor. The teacher of this class had been a personal student of the famous teacher Emma Curtis Hopkins, in Chicago. This teacher in Colorado often talked to those gathered about the "omnipresence" of God and God's goodness and how they could claim it through spoken words.

At those weekly meetings, this teacher gave the students specific affirmations on the omnipresence of God. She asked them to deliberately speak forth those words at home and during the day as they worked.

The young woman from Kentucky had a traditional religious background and such theory about words was new to her. Yet she decided to try it because she had a painful throat condition for which doctors had been unable to find a remedy. She was in pain most of the time and unable to eat normally.

One day in class as the teacher was affirming omnipresence for those in attendance, the student from Kentucky suddenly realized she had just been healed. She could swallow without pain and she "knew" she was all right. That night, as her doubting family looked on, she ate a normal meal for the first time in months.

When she proudly told her teacher of her healing at the next meeting, her teacher replied matter-of-factly, "Of course you've been healed." Because the teacher knew the power of words, such healings were a common occurrence in her work.

This young woman who was healed through affirmations continued using her gift of prophecy to help others. Her name was Nona Brooks, and she became the founder of the Divine Science movement in Denver. She served as president of its college and minister of its mother church, where she worked for many years. To those who know the result-getting power of words, she has become a legend.

## HOW TO PROPHESY WITH WORDS

You cut out your destiny with your words.

Here is a simple method for developing your gift of prophecy. Set aside a definite time every day and speak forth bold words of good, describing your life as you want it to be. If you persistently speak forth such words, even if you do not believe what they mean at first, you will find that your words have power. As you continue to speak them forth every day, your words will work miracles in your life—sometimes slowly, sometimes suddenly.

*When you speak forth constructive words every day, you are not trying to make God give you anything. You are only claiming that which is already your heritage: increased health, wealth, and happiness.*

I invite you to prophesy the good for yourself and others often, both casually and deliberately. Do not strain or become tense in your words, but declare them in peace, joy, and confidence. Then release your prophetic words to go forth into the ethers to do their perfect work for you and others. You may wish to begin right now by prophesying:

AS I CHANGE MY WORDS, I CHANGE MY WORLD.

AS I IMPROVE MY WORDS, I IMPROVE MY WORLD.

AS I TRANSFORM MY WORDS, I TRANSFORM MY WORLD.

I PROPHESY THE GOOD NOW—FOR MYSELF AND FOR ALL HUMANITY.

## PART II:
## PROPHECY THROUGH PICTURES

Prophecy—"a declaration of something to come"—does not necessarily require words. How can you have a prophecy without words?

In another simple way—through the imagination . . . as you deliberately *picture* the good you want to bring into your life. *If you do not deliberately picture what you want in a constructive way, you unconsciously picture what you do not want in a de-*

*structive way. You are always picturing something because it
is the function of the mind to picture.*

A wise way to prophesy through pictures is by asking for
guidance about your future. Through the strong hunches and
deep-seated desires that well up within you, you will intuitively
be shown what to picture. Then boldly get busy doing so.

Dr. Raymond Barker has explained it in his book *The Science of Successful Living*:*

> God wants you to be what you want to be. In your quiet
> thinking select your future, accept it as normal for you, and
> then expect it to happen. Give thanks that the ways and
> means to bring it to pass are already in action.

You must mentally accept in the present what you actually
want to happen in the future. Picturing it brings that acceptance
much quicker.

Why?

Because the picturing power of the mind turns your thinking from "I cannot have this" or "It will never happen to me"
to hope and belief and finally to the mental acceptance that "It
can happen to me" and "It will happen to me."

Generalities do not produce results because they lack substance and power. Vague hopes and indefinite goals are not
convincing to the mind and do not produce constructive results,
whereas a clear-cut picture of the good you want activates people, places, and events to cooperate with your pictured desires.

*You can hasten your good through picturing it!*

---

* Published by Dodd, Mead & Company, New York, 1966, copyright by Dr.
Raymond Charles Barker.

## HOW AN INSURANCE COMPANY SUCCEEDS
## THROUGH PICTURING

Knowing this, the president of an insurance company hastened the success of his company through picturing it.

When he formed his company, he made a "success map" on which he charted out the desired sales for his company over a ten-year period. For each year during those ten years, he listed on his chart the income he wished his company to make.

At the time he showed me his success map, the company's income was one year ahead of that pictured on his chart, although this was in the midst of a severe recession, when no one was supposed to be prospering.

## HOW PICTURING BROUGHT $500

Instead of fighting problems, you can picture your way out of them. A woman desperately needed $500 with which to meet certain financial obligations that were coming due. On the wall of her family room, she placed a "success map" she made using a piece of bright poster board.

As she daily looked at several pictures of financial goals on her success map and gave thanks for quick results, her method worked. Within ten days, three of the pictured goals came to pass and she removed those pictures and added new ones.

One of her goals had been for $500 in cash. Only a week after placing that amount on the success map, a man she had not seen in fifteen years knocked at her door and presented her with a check for exactly $500! He explained that it represented some old, cancelled insurance policies. Through a change in company rules, her formerly cancelled endowment plan had been converted to a twenty-year term insurance plan. The check he handed her was in payment.

## HOW PICTURING BROUGHT HER "SCRAPBOOK HUSBAND"

*Picture your good and bring it through, rather than trying to force it through or even reason it through. All the forces of heaven and earth will get busy cooperating with your pictures and will help bring them to pass.*

Many people have pictured vacations, better jobs, increased incomes, the healing of health problems, the sale of homes and businesses, the loss of weight, freedom from the desire to smoke or drink. Picturing can free you from all kinds of problems, both large and small.

A young woman learned of the power of pictures and made a marriage scrapbook. The pictures in her scrapbook included those of the man of her dreams, an engagement ring, wedding clothes, many showers and parties, a beautiful wedding, and a happy marriage.

Her method worked. She met her dream man and was soon wearing his engagement ring. Later her numerous showers and parties were the talk of the town, as was her trousseau. Her wedding was as beautiful as the one she pictured. A few years ago, she proudly introduced me to her "scrapbook husband" in Atlanta, Georgia, where they are busy living "happily ever after."

## HOW HAPPINESS, CONTENTMENT, AND PROSPERITY CAME TO A BUSINESSMAN

A businessman from Ohio recently wrote:

Having been a tool and machine designer most of my life and dealing in mathematics and cold facts, there is nothing of much use to me if it does not work. I have found and proven to myself that having unshakeable faith, a definite purpose or desire, and the willingness to abide with these principles, plus the faith that God will work all things out for your good, is just as sound a formula as any mathematical, chemical, or physical law.

We do not stop to figure out why two plus two equals four every time we want to work a mathematical problem. We accept it with unmistakable faith. We also have to accept the laws of life the same way.

I was first introduced to this philosophy by the engineer who was in Dr. Ponder's first prosperity class in Alabama in 1958. He went from a million-dollar construction job in Alabama to a fifteen-million dollar construction job in Ohio as a result of that prosperity class. He is the man who designed the Wheel of Fortune about which she writes in several of her books, including *Open Your Mind to Prosperity*, *The Dynamic Laws of Prosperity*, and *The Millionaires of Genesis*.*

Tragic experiences had brought me to my knees mentally, physically, and financially, when I was introduced to prosperous thinking by this man. He suggested I make a Wheel of Fortune picturing the good I wished to experience in my life. He explained picturing as "prayer in pictures," an act of faith. I followed his advice.

The results? *I am now more happy, content, independent, and prosperous than at any time in my life!* Many things began to happen right out of the blue that I didn't believe were possible. Positions opened up at just the right time, money began to flow my way, people became more helpful,

---

* Instructions for making a Wheel of Fortune are found in these books.

and even parking spaces opened up at the right time. Picturing works!

Begin to prophesy the good through picturing it. As you do so, declare often: "I NOW MOVE FORWARD INTO MY EXPANDED GOOD—DIVINELY DIRECTED AND LAVISHLY PROSPERED. ALL THINGS CONFORM TO THE RIGHT THING FOR ME NOW, QUICKLY AND IN PEACE."

# YOUR GIFT OF "NOTHING BUT THE BEST"

## — Chapter 4 —

Releasing the old, speaking words for new good, and picturing it are all specific ways for opening your mind to receive. There is also a basic overall method for doing so. It is found in this popular jingle: "GOOD, BETTER, BEST. I WILL NEVER LET IT REST, UNTIL MY GOOD IS BETTER, AND MY BETTER IS BEST!"

People have often been conditioned to *expect* less than the best and to *settle* for less than the best in life.

Part of this conditioning goes back to an erroneous belief about the nature of God and people, and their relationship. If you have believed that God has a split personality of good and evil, and that people are sinners and are thereby limited in every way, then of course you have been conditioned to settle for less than the best in life. You didn't dare to claim anything more!

But when we learn the unlimited Truth about God's goodness and its availability to everyone, we are set free from such limited beliefs and from the limited results of those beliefs.

I have found it worthwhile to declare often as I go about my day: "NOTHING BUT THE BEST." This helps me open my mind to receive in an overall way. Once while vacationing in an unfamiliar area with friends, we entered a crowded, noisy restaurant. Our first thought was whether we should remain and wait in line. "Nothing but the best" was our decision.

Since this situation was not "the best" for us, we moved on. We quickly found a picturesque restaurant overlooking the water, with quaint surroundings, excellent food, and attentive service. There was none of the noise or feeling of being crowded we found in the previous restaurant. We would not have discovered and enjoyed this unusual place if we had settled for less than the best.

## HOW A WIDOW PROSPERS

When we realize that we live in a universe of unlimited good and that a loving God wants us to share in that vast good, then we no longer feel guilty about daring to expect the best in life and *to hold out for it*.

Our beliefs about God and humanity can lead either to a dismal existence or to our accepting and claiming the best in life. This report came from the State of Washington:

My husband had just passed away. I was fifty-four years old and I realize now, in looking back, that I was accepting considerable limitation. I sold our home and moved into our small summer house. I talked about cutting back on my expenses in order to live on a "fixed income." I also accepted the fact that my credit would be more limited than when I was married.

All of this limited thinking was dumb. Really dumb! In the last three years, I have become managing broker of a real estate office with six salesmen licensed to work with me. I have obtained a new mortgage in my name and on my credit reputation. I have paid off some property on which we owed. I bought a nice new car with all the extras.

These tangible blessings plus an inner sense of harmony came to me not because of added ability but because I began to expect a better life. "I AM THE RICH CHILD OF A LOVING GOD" were the words I used daily to reassure myself that I deserved these things and more.

## HOW A LAWYER PASSED HIS BAR EXAM

A young lawyer explained how he passed his bar exam and went into a successful practice in the hill country of Texas after he conditioned himself mentally to accept his spiritual heritage of "nothing but the best."
He wrote:

On December 21, 1971, I graduated from law school. During that holiday season the excitement of finally graduating was extinguished by apprehension about passing the bar exam. Even though I was a law graduate, if I did not pass, I would not be admitted to practice after three years of hard work.

On January 3, 1972, I began attending the thirty-day bar-review course prior to taking the exam. During the first three weeks of that course, I studied on the average of fifteen hours a day, but I felt inside that I would not be able to pass. My wife, who worked as hard as I did to get me through law school, and our children were depending on my passing the bar exam. All future employment depended on it and I did not have the self-confidence to endure this terrific pressure. By the end of the third week of the review course, I was about to lose my sanity and was mentally exhausted.

That weekend, my mother paid us a visit and gave me a copy of the Ponder book *The Dynamic Laws of Prosperity.* I seldom read anything Mother gives us since our literary tastes are so different. But for some reason I sat down on our front porch and began studying that book. It is hard to describe what took place within me as I read that prosperity and success were my heritage and that I should expect and claim them. In a short time, these ideas re-established my self-confidence. When I finished reading that book, I felt as if a huge weight had been lifted from my shoulders. When I attended another session of the review course the next day, I was amazed at how confident I had become.

Well, I passed the exam and was admitted to the State Bar on April 20, 1972. In August I was employed by a law firm in the southern part of the state to open and manage a new branch office here in the scenic hill country of central Texas. It was the exact job I had been praying for, because it allows me to practice law on my own, live in a small country town, and still have a decent salary. All of these blessings came after I realized that the best was none too good for me as a child of God.

## THE RESULTS OF A "FIRST-CLASS CONSCIOUSNESS"

Once a young man in college used that old cliché, "It only costs a little more to go first-class." The results were that everything worked out well for him. He was blessed with a lovely wife, nice children, a comfortable home, a fine job, and good health. He developed a life of satisfaction and fulfillment as he held to this theme.

## HOW A REALTOR PROSPERED

Certainly the Master Teacher had a "first-class consciousness" twenty centuries ago. Jesus not only had a great prayer consciousness and a great healing consciousness, but He also had a consciousness of "nothing but the best," as is evidenced through His prosperity miracles and prosperity parables. *

Among His many promises was this familiar one: "In my Father's house are many mansions." (John 14:2) A realtor meditated upon this prosperity promise of Jesus and received two new real estate listings the next day!

## HOW TO CLAIM THE BEST

Perhaps you are thinking, "How do I claim 'nothing but the best' in my life experiences? How can I help to bring this about?"

An affirmation that has worked miracles for many people is: "GOD IS SO GOOD, LIFE IS SO WONDERFUL, AND I AM SO RICHLY BLESSED." Just thinking in this way helps us to open our minds to the best in life.

Another statement that has helped me over the years to expand the good in my world is: "I HAVE A DIVINE RIGHT TO THE BEST. I NOW TRUST MY DIVINE RIGHT TO BRING ME OUT RIGHT IN EXPERIENCING THE BEST."

As you make these statements your "prosperity vow," you become rich from the inside out!

## THE PRIESTS WERE MILLIONAIRES

That we should have nothing but the best has a strong biblical basis. The priests of the Old Testament were millionaires. It was decreed that they should be lavishly provided for under

---

* See *The Millionaire from Nazareth.*

Mosaic law, which was given to Moses by Jehovah right out of the ethers. (Numbers 18:21-32)

When the Promised Land was divided, eleven of the tribes of Israel were given *all* of the Promised Land. The twelfth priestly tribe, the Levites, was given *none* of the Promised Land. Instead they were to receive from the other eleven tribes all of the *tithes* from the Promised Land. From those tithes the Levites were instructed to share a "tithe of the tithe," known as a "heave offering" (Numbers 18:26), with the tabernacle and later with the temple. Through this method both the priests and places of worship were lavishly provided for.* The priests were adorned in the finest garments and jewels. (Exodus 28, 29) The places of worship were decorated in the finest of woods, fabrics, and gold. (Exodus 25, 26, 27)

Perhaps the reason a loving God decreed that the priests should be so well supported by tithes from the rich Promised Land was that the priests needed to be freed from all earthly and material care, so they would have time to grow spiritually and lead their followers forward on the spiritual path.

As children of God, we are also, in a sense, priests. Developing a prosperous consciousness frees us from being bound to a material existence, so we too are free to grow spiritually and to help others.

## THE PURITANS STRESSED A BELIEF IN PROSPERITY

Prosperity is not only our spiritual heritage but it is our national heritage as well! The early Puritans believed we were put on Earth to use our talents fully and to prosper—that this

---

* For a more complete description of their prosperity during that period, see Chapter 7 of the Ponder book, *The Millionaire Moses*.

was God's will. They believed that not to prosper was a sign of God's disfavor.

We help to expand the vision the early founding fathers had for America (and for the world) when we expect the best, thereby prospering.

## HOW A SCHOOLTEACHER OBTAINED THE BEST

*We should expect the best and so live that the best may become part of our experience. When we dare to do this, we often make remarkable progress in a very short length of time!*

It matters not what you have experienced in the past. If you will begin this very moment expecting the best, your very expectancy will cause you to make remarkable progress quickly!

Expecting the best works on all levels of life. There once was a schoolteacher who always expected her students to do well in her classes, and they did. Those same students often did not do well in other classes, but they did so for this woman. She expected it, and it happened repeatedly.

The German poet and philosopher Goethe said, "Treat people as if they were what they ought to be, and you will help them become what they are capable of becoming." This lady proved it.

An experiment was conducted in one school recently. Students from kindergarten through the fifth grade were placed under certain teachers. These teachers were told that these particular students were exceptionally brilliant, although the students were not really brilliant. They were simply normal.

Nevertheless, these normal students made brilliant marks in school that year. Also, they were far happier than the children around them.

Why? They responded to the positive expectations of their instructors. When the teachers considered them the best of students, they became so.

When we dare to expect the best for ourselves and for others, we open the way for the best to come to us, often quickly. In any event, we make tremendous progress just by thinking in this way: "NOTHING BUT THE BEST."

## HOW A DOCTOR BROUGHT ABOUT
## REMARKABLE HEALINGS

There once was a doctor who was able to heal many patients who had been elsewhere and had not been healed. He had no unusual scholastic record in medical school and had been a very ordinary medical student.

Yet when people came to him, even after seeking help elsewhere, they were often healed quickly. An investigation revealed why: He expected the best for his patients.

He would even tell those who seemed to be dying that there was no reason for them not to get well right away. Often they did. He frequently said to people, "You can get well—because you are better than you thought you were." These constructive words caused his patients to expect the best. And this method worked.

## A NURSE OBSERVES THAT
## ATTITUDES DETERMINE RECOVERY

A nurse in San Antonio, Texas, once said, "We can usually tell by a person's attitude on the day he is admitted on this floor of the hospital how long it will take him to get well.

"Everyone on this floor has essentially the same health problem. When they go to surgery, they go for basically the same operation. By all normal standards, they should all get well and go home in about the same length of time. But it doesn't work out that way."

She continued, "I made a discovery when I came into the nursing profession twenty years ago. I quickly realized that attitudes determine a patient's recovery time. When a person admitted on this floor gives us a hard time, is unpleasant or difficult to deal with, and is making a big thing of his illness, we can be sure his operation will be difficult and his recovery slow. But if he is pleasant, harmonious, cooperative, and is thinking in terms of getting well, then his operation is uneventful and his recovery rapid."

She concluded, "Some people go home after surgery in five to seven days. They are the positive thinkers. Some go home in ten days to two weeks. They are less positive. Some go home in about three weeks and 'enjoy ill health' for the rest of their lives. They are the negative thinkers. It all depends on what they expect."

## HOW A NEW JOB AND A NEW MARRIAGE CAME

There once was a widow of fifty-two who was bored with her menial, low-paying job. Then she learned that she could have whatever she expected. She learned that if she would expect the best, it would still come to her, regardless of age or station in life.

This widow decided to find out if expecting the best really worked. She made a list of the blessings she would like to have: a better job, a happier life, even another marriage.

Soon after she began thinking along these lines, someone told her that the state of Alaska was a place of great opportunity. She wrote the largest newspaper in Alaska and inquired.

The manager of the paper wrote her a personal reply and urged her to come to Alaska; at that time, there were plenty of jobs and no age barrier. She packed up and moved to Alaska, where she soon found a stenographer's job.

Six months later she married a fine man and settled happily. Later she said, "I relate this experience because so many people complain about tough luck, bad breaks, unforeseen circumstances, getting old, and so on. If people would expect the best in life instead of expecting tough luck and bad breaks, the tide could turn for them."

This woman then gave the affirmations she had used to help turn the tide in her life: "TODAY AND EVERY DAY I EXPECT THE BEST. WONDERFUL THINGS ARE HAPPENING TO ME NOW. EVERYTHING I DO TURNS INTO GOOD FOR MYSELF AND OTHERS." Often she would say: "WONDERFUL THINGS ARE BOUND TO HAPPEN." And they did.

A noted speaker recently said, "No one should go through life a beggar when he can be a king." This woman—"later in life"—had proved it.

## MEDITATION UPON THE BEST BRINGS THE BEST

In claiming your gift of "nothing but the best," a fine way to begin is by meditating daily upon these words: "AS A CHILD OF GOD, I HAVE A DIVINE RIGHT TO THE BEST. I NOW EXPECT THE BEST. I SO LIVE THAT THE BEST MAY BECOME A PART OF MY EXPERIENCE. WHEN I DARE TO EXPECT THE BEST, I MAKE REMARKABLE PROGRESS QUICKLY. EXPECTING THE BEST FOR OTHERS PRODUCES REMARKABLE GOOD FOR THEM, TOO. TODAY AND EVERY DAY, I EXPECT THE BEST. WONDERFUL THINGS HAPPEN TO ME NOW, AS I CLAIM MY SPIRITUAL HERITAGE OF 'NOTHING BUT THE BEST.'"

# YOUR GIFT OF A "PEOPLE CONSCIOUSNESS"

## Chapter 5

A newspaper item read, "Too many people are trying to solve the problems of the world when they haven't straightened out their own lives." How true. The frustrations of the world would more easily be resolved if we first resolved the frustrations in our own lives.

As a spiritual being, made in the image and likeness of God, you have dominion over your world. This means you have freedom concerning the kinds of people who come into your world and who leave it. You have freedom to change your world. If you do not like your world, or the people in it, you can do something about it, because you have been given the gift of a "people consciousness."

Most people have thought just the opposite: that there is nothing they can do about their world or the people in it. They have helplessly thought they must tolerate and suffer having uncongenial people in their lives.

It is not true! You can effect changes by first changing your people consciousness: your attitudes about people. Your consciousness (thought and feeling nature) is the result of the ideas you have *held* in mind. You can change your consciousness by changing the ideas you are *holding* to mentally and emotionally.

*Instead of trying to change the people in your world, you should work to change your thoughts and feelings about those people.* When you do that, the people in your world either respond harmoniously or move out of your life and find their good elsewhere. Everyone involved is satisfied and blessed.

## THE LAW OF ATTRACTION

All of the people in your world are there through the law of attraction. Either consciously or subconsciously, you have attracted them through your thoughts and feelings, either in this life or perhaps some other time.

Some mystics claim that everyone you meet is someone you have known before. They claim that the bonds of love or hate have attracted into your life people from the past. They feel you are together again by divine appointment to learn lessons and to complete emotional assignments.

In any event, all of your problems and all of your blessings are related to people, so *developing your people consciousness is one of the greatest things you can do to improve your world.*

You have probably heard that quip, "I love life. I just can't stand people." When you are concerned about the people in your world, remind yourself often that "NO PERSON, THING, OR EVENT CAN KEEP FROM ME THAT WHICH THE UNIVERSE HAS FOR ME NOW. ALL THAT HAS BEEN DONE AGAINST ME NOW HELPS ME."

## THE WIDOW WHO DIDN'T WANT
## FREEDOM FROM LONELINESS

There are those who often gripe about the people in their world. Yet when they are given an opportunity to bring new people into their lives, these gripers refuse to do so. They enjoy their "people problems." They do not want freedom from them.

I once knew a lady who was widowed and very lonely. She would often come to see me in the church where I served. She said she wanted something to do with her life besides visiting among her children and their families. We prayed and asked God to bring some new people into her life and God did.

One day a member of our church introduced her to his widowed brother. They discovered they had many common interests. Both were financially independent and in good health.

When this man asked this widow to marry him, she declined, even though she had thought that was what she wanted. Her reason? He was in his seventies. She was in her sixties. Yet she said *he* was "too old" for *her*!

A loving God had tried to answer her prayer, but this widow did not want to change her people consciousness. She just wanted something to complain about. She has continued to live alone and to claim she doesn't like it, but don't you believe it!

## DEVELOPING A PEOPLE CONSCIOUSNESS
## MAY BRING CHANGES

God is the source of all your good, but God uses people as channels for bringing blessings to you.

It is both humbling and inspiring to realize how much of our good comes to us through other people. It is also humbling, though not so inspiring, to realize *how often we have cut off the channels to our good by not appreciating the people who are already in our lives.*

We have also cut off the channels to our good by not opening our minds to the possibility of new people entering our lives, people who would bring with them many new blessings for us.

I once found myself acting as guest minister in a sleepy little ministry, so I did a number of things to try to wake up the church and help it grow. But when it did begin to grow, the members of long standing resented the growth. They disliked the new people who appeared. They said, "Now when I come to church, I don't see anybody I know. I only see all of those 'new people.'"

There's nothing unusual about this attitude. Most of us are inclined to resent new people who come into our lives in the midst of other changes, even when they come to help clear away our problems and to bless us.

## WHY PROBLEM PEOPLE ARE IN OUR LIVES

What about our people consciousness? How can we deliberately develop our people consciousness so it includes happy, harmonious, progressive individuals to whom we are attuned? How can we clear out of our lives the "dead wood"—those problem people to whom we are not attuned, whose association with us has run its course in our lives?

*Problem people are in our lives by divine appointment, though the appointment may not seem to be divine.* Problem people are in our lives because we have attracted them to us for one of two reasons:

*First*. Problem people are in our lives so we may bless them.

*Second*. Problem people are in our lives so we may learn something from them.

If we resent problem people, fight with them, or criticize them, we just hold them in our lives by our own strong negative emotions. Most of us have done this.

But if we realize that problem people are in our lives by divine appointment—so we may bless them or so we may learn something from them—then it's easier for us to get the job done and be free to go our own way into new, happier relationships.

Instead of resenting and criticizing the problem people that cross your path, say to them mentally: "YOU ARE IN MY LIFE BY DIVINE APPOINTMENT. YOU HAVE CROSSED MY PATH SO I MAY LEARN SOMETHING FROM YOU. YOU HAVE CROSSED MY PATH TO RECEIVE MY BLESSING. I FREELY GIVE YOU MY BLESSING AND I NOW RELEASE YOU TO YOUR HIGHEST GOOD ELSEWHERE."

Just thinking in this way takes the sting out of unhappy relationships and begins to make them right.

## HOW THE AUTHOR WAS FREED
## FROM PROBLEM PEOPLE

I once found myself surrounded by uncongenial people with whom I had nothing in common. Nothing worked to free me from those people as long as I condemned them. My criticism bound me even more strongly to them.

But the moment I began to bless them as a part of my good, they responded. I was soon freed from that set of circum-

stances through the offer of another job and through the natural
outworking of events. But no new doors opened to me until I
began to bless instead of criticize those who had concerned me.

## SPEAK THE WORD OF RELEASE

Too many of us spend time resisting, resenting, and mentally fighting the people in our world, when those people
would leave our world quickly if we would only speak the
word of release for them.

An effective release statement is this: "GOD BRINGS INTO
MY LIFE THE RIGHT PEOPLE WHO CAN HELP ME AND MAKE ME
HAPPY, AND WHOM I CAN HELP AND MAKE HAPPY. THOSE PEO-
PLE WHO ARE NO LONGER FOR MY HIGHEST GOOD NOW FADE
OUT OF MY LIFE AND FIND THEIR GOOD ELSEWHERE. I BLESS
THEM ON THEIR WAY."

A woman was desperately unhappy in her marriage but felt
bound to it because of her six children. When she learned of
the power there is in speaking the word of release for inharmonious relationships in one's life, she decided to try it. She daily
declared: "MY LIFE CANNOT BE LIMITED. CHRIST IN ME NOW
FREES ME FROM ALL LIMITATION. I AM UNFETTERED AND UN-
BOUND. I AM IN TRUE RELATIONSHIP WITH ALL PEOPLE AND ALL
SITUATIONS NOW."

Although daily use of these statements gave her a sense of
hope, they did not free her from an unhappy marriage. Even
when her relationship with her husband became more harmonious, she continued to feel their marriage had run its course.

Then she learned that there is power in speaking words that
will free the people in your life. She learned that as you free
them, those who should remain in your life will do so. Those
who should clear out of your life will do so in peace.

She began to use these definite release statements every day: "I NOW RELEASE AND AM RELEASED FROM EVERYTHING AND EVERYBODY WHO IS NO LONGER A PART OF THE DIVINE PLAN OF MY LIFE. EVERYTHING AND EVERYBODY WHO IS NO LONGER A PART OF THE DIVINE PLAN OF MY LIFE NOW RELEASES ME AND FINDS THEIR GOOD ELSEWHERE. I NOW EXPAND QUICKLY INTO THE DIVINE PLAN OF MY LIFE, WHERE ALL CONDITIONS ARE PERMANENTLY PERFECT."

Her husband soon agreed to a divorce. This was something he had said he would never do. The divorce action took place so quietly that few people knew anything about it. Upon its completion, she took her six children home to visit her parents in another state. On that visit she met a fine man whom she soon married.

As for her six children, her new husband was glad to have them on his ranch, where they proved to be a blessing in many ways. This expanded new life worked out happily for everyone involved.

But none of it came about until this previously unhappy woman had spoken words that released the inharmonious relationships in her life.

## RELEASE THE PEOPLE YOU LOVE, TOO

It may not be the people you dislike, but the ones you love the most who cause your people problems. Through their love for you and their emotional ties to you, there sometimes exists a sense of possessiveness, of being dominated, of not being free, which can cause people problems. Inharmonious family relationships often reflect this.

When you feel bound by the people you love, that is the time to declare: "MY LIFE CANNOT BE LIMITED. CHRIST IN ME

NOW FREES ME FROM ALL LIMITATIONS. I AM UNFETTERED AND
UNBOUND."

You can experience freedom with the people you love by
declaring often: "I LOVE ALL PEOPLE AND ALL PEOPLE LOVE ME
WITHOUT ATTACHMENT." People who have attached themselves
to you unduly will find other interests and will move out of
your life naturally. Your relationships with them will become
more balanced and more free, so you can enjoy them again.

## EMOTIONAL FREEDOM OFTEN LEADS TO CHANGE

There may be surprises when you start speaking the word
of freedom from attachment. The decision to let go that which
has completed its course in your life usually leads to change.

Many human ills are caused by our unwisely binding people and things to us, or our letting people and things unwisely
bind us to them. All of our loosing is not simply loosing that
which has become troublesome. Good is seldom static. It is
progressive. It evolves and changes, and we must evolve and
change with it. We must loosen accustomed forms of good
when our progress or that of someone else involved demands
it. As soon as we do so, nothing can take from us that which
still belongs to us by divine right.

## HOW TO GAIN FREEDOM
## FROM THE OPINIONS OF OTHERS

In claiming our freedom, we must loose other people's
opinions of what we should or should not do. *When we learn to
claim our freedom from human opinion, most of our problems
can be resolved.* (Of course we should seek professional advice
on technical matters from our doctor, lawyer, accountant, bro-

ker, realtor, or banker. But we should then evaluate that advice, leaning heavily upon our inner feelings about what is best for us.)

We also learn not to tell other people what they should or should not do. They have a divine intelligence within them to guide them. It is wise to pray for that divine intelligence to show them the way. When tempted to give or receive unsolicited advice, declare: "I PRONOUNCE YOU FREE FROM THE OPINIONS OF OTHERS. I PRONOUNCE MYSELF FREE FROM THE OPINIONS OF OTHERS. ALL THINGS CONFORM TO THE RIGHT THING NOW, QUICKLY AND IN PEACE."

## HOW A DOCTOR PROVED THAT
## THE GOOD OF ONE IS THE GOOD OF ALL

You can gain freedom from other people's opinions by realizing that whatever most completely satisfies your own inner feelings is that which is best for you and for everyone concerned. "The good of one is the good of all" is an old proverb.

A mother had worked long and hard to get her son through school, including medical college. When he set up a small practice in his home town, he did well. Later he was offered an opportunity to study in Europe with a famous psychiatrist. He hesitated to accept the offer because it would mean leaving his mother alone for a long period.

Her friends said, "What a selfish son you have. After all you have done for him, now he's thinking of leaving you alone while he has a good time abroad."

You may know something of the guilt that people try to inflict upon you when they decide you are being selfish by *their* standards. This young doctor wisely determined that both his and his mother's lives would be improved for his having studied abroad, and he went.

His mother was very lonely but gradually she made her adjustment. When her son returned, he became a successful psychiatrist and was able to provide her with far more than she ever dreamed they would have. She found herself happier than she had thought possible.

This young doctor proved that *if a thing is good for you, in the long run it is good for everyone involved.* If a thing is not right for you, in the long run it is not right for anyone involved.

Many of your people problems would be solved if you would stop trying to please other people unduly. Stop catering to the opinions of others. Start thinking about what is right for you. What is right for you is also right for others. Never mind "what people think." The point is, what do you think?

If you do what is best for you, it will also be best for everyone else. The course of action that makes you feel right inside is your highest good. Take it. Your only obligation is to the Spirit of Truth within you. This is the yardstick to follow when your loyalties have become confused.

## WHAT IS RIGHT GIVES YOU A SENSE OF PEACE

The way to be sure you do what is right for you is to do that which gives you a sense of peace.

*Whatever gives you a sense of struggle and strife is false. Whatever gives you a sense of peace is right.* Once when I had a people problem that I struggled within myself to solve, nothing worked out. As I thought about the problem, I got only a sense of strife. Finally, I blessed the people involved and mentally released them in peace. My prayer statement was simply: "I BLESS YOU AND RELEASE YOU IN PEACE."

That method worked. Those people quickly moved out of my life. Months later, when I saw them again, everything was peaceful and right.

So whatever gives you a sense of peace is the thing to do. Whatever gives you a sense of strife and mental struggle is the thing *not* to do. As you declare "I BLESS YOU AND RELEASE YOU IN PEACE," this opens the way for the situation to right itself. *People and situations often right themselves when we bless them and free them.*

## WHAT YOU CAN DO TO BE HAPPY

Another way to develop a happy people consciousness is to take a stand in your thinking about your life and the people in it. Say to yourself: "I HAVE A RIGHT TO BE HAPPY AND I CLAIM MY HAPPINESS NOW."

Then stop complaining. Stop telling others of your people problems. Start looking for the good points in relatives, friends, and coworkers. When anyone asks you how things are, declare the Truth as it is on the inner plane. Tell them that things are getting better all the time, that you feel great, and that life is wonderful.

Stop discussing what you do *not* want. Stop discussing the people who have made you unhappy. Stop feeding unpleasant situations with your negative talk. This only keeps them alive.

Start doing new and different things. Activate your social life. Expand your circle of friends, but do it in a certain way. Clear out of your life socially those people who do not uplift and inspire you. They can do you no good.

Deliberately bring into your life socially other people who think and believe as you do. They can be constructive friends to you. Stop compromising with the types of people you allow

in your world socially. You may have to work with people you
do not like—at least until you straighten out your people consciousness—but you do not have to socialize with them. Relax
only with happy, constructive people.

Here is the reason this is so important: when you are relaxed, suggestions are absorbed by your subconscious mind
much quicker. Those suggestions, either positive or negative,
manifest results in your life very quickly. Because of this you
should relax only with happy people who think and speak constructively.

You meet three kinds of people in life: *first*, those you can
help; *second*, those who are on your same level mentally, emotionally, and economically; *third*, those who can help you.

When you are relaxing, be sure to do so with one of the last
two categories. Do not allow yourself to be drained mentally or
emotionally by trying to relax with those who need your help.
As a part of your humanitarian efforts, you may wish to aid
people in this category in whatever ways seem appropriate to
you. But do not try to relax with them. To do so is a "strenuous" way to relax, and it is always disappointing. What you
mean to be a time of relaxation becomes a time of work. Since
it is a time of unofficial work, you won't be paid for your time
or efforts.

## HOW THE AUTHOR BROUGHT
## NEW PEOPLE INTO HER LIFE

During a period when I desperately needed some new people in the church where I served and when I needed new personal friends, I quietly made a "people map." On a piece of
big, beautiful, rose-colored poster board, I placed pictures of

happy people. There were young people, retired people, and many pictures of happily married couples.

Within a few weeks from the time I started daily viewing my people map, I realized that new people were appearing in my world. Within six months my world was filled with many new people who seemed just right for it. Some of my best friends came into my life during that period.

## BRIGHTEN UP YOUR WORLD

Brighten up yourself. Brighten up your home and office. Get into circulation more. Find things to be happy about. Remind yourself often: "A LOVING GOD WANTS ME TO BE HAPPIER THAN I HAVE EVER BEEN BEFORE! I HAVE A DIVINE RIGHT TO BE HAPPY, SO I CLAIM MY HAPPINESS NOW." Then open the channels of your life to receive new people and new good. The results can amaze you. What a wonderful way to open your mind to receive.

# YOUR GIFT OF GROWTH AND EXPANSION

— Chapter 6 —

The word "grow" means "to expand," "to increase in size," or "to develop toward maturity."

You have been given the gift of growth and expansion. It is a part of your heritage of unlimited good. By understanding the process of growth, you can more easily accept your good and expand it more quickly.

Everyone is growing toward maturity, though they may not know it. Once you put your foot on the inner path and learn about the power of thought as a tool for your good, your growth can be accelerated. Learning this will help you recognize and understand the phases through which you shall pass, so your growth can be unaccompanied by pain.

## THE THREE PHASES OF YOUR GROWTH

The process of inner growth or expansion into your good is much the same as the process of physical growth. There are basically three phases through which you grow into your expanded good.

*First*, there is the time of planting the seed.

On the inner plane, this is the time of planting the idea of good in your thoughts and feelings, in preparation for its manifestation in your life. Most of the ideas expressed earlier in this book are given for that purpose.

This is an active period in which you are doing something. You are busy deliberately planting the idea of good in your thought and feeling nature. During this time you may be reading inspirational and self-help books. Perhaps you are decreeing good words and holding good thoughts. You may be planning the way you want your life to be in pictures on a success map and through list-making.

During such a period it is wise to attend related classes and lectures. You will want to associate with other people who think and talk constructively. You will want to put God first financially by consistently tithing, thereby invoking "ten, the magic number of increase." In every possible way you will want to increase the thought of good in your life. Offering these ideas to others can be helpful, too.

As you do these things, you begin to feel consciously in control and in charge of your world. You feel the inner and outer expansion begin to slowly take place.

*Second*, there is the time of waiting for the crop of new good to grow.

This is the period when you are waiting for your seed-idea of expanded good to take root and grow in the invisible until it breaks through the hard thoughts, feelings, and conditions of the past. At this time you will want to remind yourself often that *there must be an inworking before there can be an outworking.*

There may be a long period in your unfoldment when you see no visible results, because you are putting your mental roots down deep—in the invisible area of the conscious mind and the subconscious mind.

This is the most trying period in the process of growth, but it is the most important, too. Many people give up at this point. Because they do not follow through, they get no further.

*Third*, there is the last period in growth, which is a time of harvest. Prayers are answered, results come. When this happens you say, "How sweet it is."

Of these three periods, the most difficult is the second when nothing seems to be happening, yet everything is happening.

How do you handle those frustrating periods in your life when you are growing inwardly but can see no outward results?

## HOW A BUSINESSMAN SUCCESSFULLY HANDLED THIS SECOND PERIOD

A businessman found out how to handle the second phase in his growth successfully—that period when nothing seemed to be happening, yet everything *was* happening.

He had purchased a new business on the outskirts of his city. He took God as his partner in this new venture, through tithing. He expected to prosper and did for a time. His new business flourished. Then suddenly, for no apparent reason, business dwindled. All of his efforts to make it prosper failed.

One night after he had closed his business for the day, he sat at his desk looking over the daily receipts. The results were so discouraging that he prayed for guidance.

Prayerfully he asked, "God, what is the truth about this situation?" The thought came, "This is a time to grow—to expand inwardly." This thought satisfied him and a great peace descended upon him.

Having been raised on a farm, this man knew of the necessity for a growing period in every process. He reminded himself that the farmer plants the seed and must let patience do its perfect work before there can be a harvest.

This businessman realized that he, too, needed time to grow. That very night he began planting a new crop of good thoughts. He started by picking up the day's receipts, along with a handful of bills he had not yet paid. He blessed them both. From the unpaid bills, he selected one he could pay right then and gladly did so. From the day's income he invested what was left in certain items for his business that sold well and had a quick turnover. He knew they would bring in quick cash.

*Instead of urging God to greater speed, he began to ask daily for divine guidance in his business transactions.* He began to pray more, to gripe and push less. He studied and meditated daily upon the infinite possibilities of good. He dwelled less upon apparent troubles.

Good things began to happen! A customer whose business he had counted on, but then lost, returned unexpectedly and brought several new customers with him. It happened again and again. Through the natural flow of events, this man's business began to prosper. He later realized he had become a far more successful person for having had a period of seasoning. He discovered that *the process of growth cannot be crowded into an instant.* His season of harvest came, in plenty of time, but only when he was ready for it, inwardly as well as outwardly.

This man discovered something we must all discover: In those quiet periods of growth, there first comes inner individual growth. Then comes outer growth and expansion in our affairs. How often we have tried to reverse the process!

We may have wanted the outer results before we've grown into them inwardly. Things are better for a period of seasoning, and so are we. A child grows without realizing it, and so do we.

## THE PROSPERING POWER OF PATIENCE

Once a poor boy, a world-famous designer now has a personal annual income of three million dollars and an annual corporate income of two hundred million dollars. When asked the secret of his success, he replied, "There is prospering power in patience. I had to learn to relax, take what came, digest it, and learn from it. If you strive too aggressively, you can scare away your good. If you want something enough, you can get it—in time—if you are willing to work for it, then wait for it. There are a lot of designers younger than myself who didn't make it and are no longer around because they were in too much of a hurry. Their impatience kept them from succeeding."

The advice given the early Christians still applies: "Let patience have its perfect work that ye may be perfect and entire, lacking in nothing." (James 1:4)

## WHY A PERIOD OF SEASONING IS NECESSARY

In my own life, I have found that some of the good things that are just now coming to me personally and professionally are blessings I thought I was ready for and should have received several decades ago. I now realize that my roots were not deep enough in the invisible to receive those blessings and maintain them. Had they come then, it would have been false growth. I would not have retained them, and I would have had to start all over again in the growth process.

Perhaps you have become accustomed to using your spoken words to decree new good, or you picture it—and expect instant results. Sometimes you have gotten them in the process. You *should* believe in "instant good" and you *should* have much more of it than you've had in the past. As you condition your mind to the possibilities of instant good, you will experience more of it in your life than ever before.

But when it does not happen to the extent you wish, remember the second phase of your growth. Be willing to grow into your expanded good in an orderly, natural way. Do not try to force it inwardly or outwardly. If you do, you may lose it. "What you fight to get, you fight to keep" is a wise truth.

## HOW A YOUNG MAN LOST HIS GOOD

I once talked with a young businessman who felt he wanted to become a minister. Over lunch he, his wife, and I discussed it. I never encourage anyone to enter the ministry nor paint them a rosy picture. It is hard work, physically, mentally, emotionally, and spiritually. It is a labor of love, but it is a labor— of the most demanding kind.

I told this young man that most ministers are grossly overworked and underpaid. For the same time in training, he could become a successful doctor or lawyer, and earn several times the income he would ever be likely to receive as a minister. It has been estimated that if the average minister, for the time and energy he or she spends working, were paid in accordance with what business executives are paid, that minister's income would be at least $200,000 a year!* (Most of the ministers I know do not make a tenth of that amount.)

But this was an aggressive young salesman who had used the power of thought successfully in his work, so he saw no reason why he should not rush headlong into the ministry. He said, "I don't need all that ministerial training. I am already a good speaker. I am ready to go out into the world as a minister right now, but 'they' will not let me."

I said, "Thank heaven, 'they' won't. It would be disastrous if 'they' did."

This young man reminded me of a tree that was all leaves and no roots. The first storm that came along would blow it over.

I talked with him about getting his zeal tempered with understanding.† It didn't make him happy when I tried to slow him down. He was in the second phase of his growth—the waiting period—and he didn't like it. But like the rest of us, he certainly needed it.

That young man would have been a far better person if he'd experienced a period of seasoning in a nonresistant way. Unfortunately, he resisted the idea completely. He soon left his own church as a member and rushed into leadership of an off-beat religious group that emphasized the power of mental force for getting results.

---

* In the years since this book was first published, salaries and prices have, of course, risen dramatically. Yet many ministers are still, by tradition, underpaid and overworked. They clearly consider their work a labor, but it is a labor of love.
† See Chapter 11, *The Healing Secrets of The Ages*, Catherine Ponder, (Camarillo, CA: DeVorss & Co., rev. ed. 1985).

The last time I heard from him was through a long-distance call from his wife. She said he had become mentally confused, emotionally upset, and physically exhausted. Of course he had!

Often we all have tended to be like this young man. We may have tried to gain the good from life without being duly prepared and properly initiated. Any effort to storm the gates of heaven can be a violation of the law of growth. Any time we violate that great law, we get a negative reaction. It often takes the form of confusion and inner disturbance. But that can be worthwhile if it slows us down to a more normal rate of development into our good.

## THERE ARE NO STRAIGHT LINES
## IN YOUR GROWTH

A secret about the fascinating law of growth is this: there are no straight lines in your growth.

People often picture progress as a straight road upon which all humanity must walk. But there is no such thing as a straight line of development anywhere in the universe. Everything moves through twists and turns and cycles, both in time and space.

The oldest universal symbol, for instance, is the circle.

The ancient Greeks said progress proceeds in a spiral, with history continually repeating itself on a higher level. What that means to you as an individual is this: regardless of the number of twists or turns or even perhaps breaks that may appear in the lines of your life, growth is still taking place.

Growth and development do not occur anywhere in nature in a straight line.

The philosopher Kahlil Gibran explained the growth process in his book *The Prophet*:

. . . the soul walks upon all paths.
The soul walks not upon a line, neither does it grow like a reed.
The soul unfolds itself, like a lotus of countless petals. *

Growth doesn't follow a straight line out. Growth doesn't follow a straight line up. You unfold into your good like a lotus of countless petals, through various experiences. Remind yourself often not to be disappointed when there seem to be no straight lines into your expanded good. You only want that good for which you have been duly prepared and properly initiated. Remember that any effort to storm the gates of heaven is a violation of the law of growth from which you can get a violent reaction. There must be an inworking before there can be an outworking, so relax into it.

## HOW TO MEET DARK PERIODS OF INITIATION

One of the ways to get initiated into your good is through meeting dark periods of your life peacefully, harmoniously, and nonresistantly. Never fight the darkness. Growth is taking place. Let it.

The divine plan for your life can grow in the darkness as well as in the light. Like grain, the divine plan for your life can grow in the rain as well as the sunny weather.

Dark periods containing challenges seem to be necessary to lift you from a static physical state into one of mental and spiri-

---

* Reprinted from *The Prophet*, by Kahlil Gibran, with permission of the publisher, Alfred A. Knopf, Inc. Copyright 1923 by Kahlil Gibran: renewal copyright 1951 by Administrators C.T.A. of Kahlil Gibran estate, and Mary G. Gibran.

tual development. *If everything you needed came to you without effort on your part, you would stagnate and die.*

By meeting and overcoming the obstacles that life presents, you are continually impelled upward. The urge to develop, to grow, and to expand your good is born within you. It is a part of your divine nature. Through life's challenges, you are forced forward on the path of growth into maturity, depth, and understanding.

The seed of divinity is within all of us. Through the dark periods in our lives, we are given the opportunity to turn within and arouse, awaken, and develop this divinity.

Dark periods are but periods of initiation into your expanded good, first on the inner plane of life. God's good purposes for your life are growing in the dark periods as well as in the happier ones. At such times declare often: "I GROW ALONG WITH MY GOOD. I FLOW ALONG WITH MY GOOD."

This is the time to give life's negative experiences the light touch. Say to yourself: "AS I GIVE IT THE LIGHT TOUCH, THIS, TOO, SHALL PASS."

## WHEN YOUR LIFE TAKES NEW DIRECTIONS, THAT'S GROWTH

A famous psychic seer recently spoke of how her life takes a complete change of direction every ten years. She said that when she had spent ten years of intensive work scientifically testing her extrasensory mind powers, she found her life taking a new direction. She then went into the publishing business and wrote on extrasensory subjects. After ten years in the field of parapsychological publishing, her life took still another direction. She left the publishing business to travel around the world lecturing on parapsychology.

As this seer realized, when your life takes a new direction, that is a part of your growth. Balance is taking place.

## WHAT TO DO WHILE AWAITING
## THE LAST PHASE OF YOUR GROWTH

When you are in that second phase of growth—the "in-working" phase—awaiting an outworking of your good, that is the time to remind yourself of this: as a progressive and growing being, you are where you are that you may learn, that you may grow.

As you learn the lesson which any circumstance contains for you, that circumstance passes away and gives place to other, better circumstances and surroundings.

How can you make the most of this period?

A magazine article once described a new process using artificial light that accelerates the growth of plants. The article described the experiments that are being conducted at a leading state university. The article was entitled "What a difference light can make in the growth of plants."

In like manner, the more light you can turn on in your life, the quicker will be your growth into your expanded good. Use the slow periods in your life for growth. Deliberately turn on the light of knowledge, truth, and understanding at those slow times. Study more. Meditate, affirm, and pray often. Dwell upon the wisdom of the universe more during those periods. Let go and trust.

## HOW TO HARVEST YOUR GOOD

As you do, the third phase of your growth will appear; the time of fulfillment and harvest will come.

When you feel it near, you can help it manifest in outward form in your life by declaring: "THE WORK OF MY HANDS AND THE PLANS OF MY LIFE ARE NOW MOVING QUICKLY TOWARD A SURE AND PERFECT FULFILLMENT. I ANTICIPATE THE GOOD. IN GOD'S RIGHT ACTION, I NOW PLACE MY FULL TRUST. THIS IS A TIME OF DIVINE COMPLETION. I NOW HARVEST MY GOOD AS MIRACLES FOLLOW MIRACLES, AND WONDERS NEVER CEASE!"

# YOUR GIFT OF PROSPEROUS INCREASE

— Chapter 7 —

The next gift I wish to share with you to help you further open your mind to receive is the gift of prosperous increase. A "gift" is a present that is tangibly or intangibly endowed. It is usually unaccompanied by hard work or strenuous effort on the part of the recipient. Instead, it may be given as an expression of friendship, affection, appreciation, or esteem.

The word "increase" means "to cause to become greater in size, amount, degree; to add to; to multiply." All normal individuals are interested in the possibility of receiving such gifts—those that are unaccompanied by hard work or strenuous effort; gifts that will cause their good to become greater and to multiply. What a delightful prospect!

## THE SECRET OF PROSPEROUS INCREASE

It has been estimated that at least thirty million people have studied self-help methods in the last decade or so, and that eighty percent of today's adult Americans are engaged in a search for self-help fulfillment. The key to whether they find that fulfillment may lie in whether they learn and apply this secret of prosperous increase.

Various schemes have been suggested for getting rich quickly. Many of them fail, because they are based on "getting"—not on "giving." Here is how the secret of prosperous increase works: systematic giving is the beginning of systematic increase. However, that giving must be done in a certain way: through consistent sharing of your tithes. The word "tithe" means "tenth," and the ancient people felt that "ten" was "the magic number of increase."

Your tithes should be given *first* and impersonally— separate from that which you spend on yourself, your family, your business, or your friends. Such impersonal gifts are usually given to religious causes, though charitable, cultural, educational, or other humanitarian causes may be included, according to one's soul growth (as explained later in this chapter).

*Systematic sharing with the universe of a portion of all that the universe shares with you is the beginning of financial increase.* Just as the farmer returns to the soil one-tenth of his seed for soil enrichment, so does impersonal giving and sharing open the way to enriched living on all levels of life to those who faithfully practice it.

Why?

Because a loving God and a rich universe are happy to multiply your good as an expression of universal affection, appreciation, and esteem. *A friendly universe always wants you to have something better than the best you are now experiencing. A loving God always wants you to be happier and more prosperous than you have ever been before!* The Creator of this lavish universe does not want you to go through life a beggar, when you should be a king. Since you are a spiritual being, made in the image and likeness of God, such blessings are your natural right. Through your consistent acts of impersonal, unselfish giving, you attune your consciousness to that of universal abundance so you put yourself in line to receive its rich gifts. This is the secret of prosperous increase.

## HOW HE DOUBLED HIS INCOME IN ONE YEAR

A businessman worked long and hard in his field, yet he never achieved the prosperity and success he felt he should have. He had taken various success courses over the years, all of which temporarily encouraged him. Yet permanent success evaded him. When he heard about the prospering power of systematic giving at a prosperity seminar, he decided to try it.

He began to tithe a tenth of his gross income on a weekly basis to the church where he had learned this prosperity principle. Every Saturday morning when he finished his workweek, he totaled up his income and wrote his tithe check *first*, before meeting other financial obligations. Within one year, his income doubled! He said the only thing he had done differently in his work during that year was to consistently give a tenth of his income to that church, of which he also became a member.

His most recent progress report included this update: he has now paid off his home mortgage, purchased a building to house his business, and taken his first vacation in years. He said simply, "Tithing spells success on all levels of life."

## HOW THE SECRET OF
## PROSPEROUS INCREASE WORKS

Systematic giving is most often done by enlightened individuals through the practice of tithing to God's work at the point or points where they are receiving spiritual help and inspiration. As previously stated, the word "tithe" means "tenth." Not only the Hebrews of the biblical era but also people of all great civilizations and cultures have felt that *ten* is the magic number of increase. They have invoked its prospering power by tithing to their priests and places of worship at least one-tenth of all they received.

The ancient Egyptians, Babylonians, Persians, Arabians, Greeks, Romans, and Chinese were among those who practiced this special method of giving. In fact, *there has never been a nation, however remote or ancient, where the practice of tithing has not prevailed.*

The Hebrews of the Old Testament became one of the richest groups of people the world has ever known because they gave not the last and the least, but the first and the best, and their giving made them rich! They never complained about their lavish giving, and they never repealed their generous tithing practices. Over and over, the payment of tithes brought them peace and plenty. *Ten* is still the magic number of increase to those who practice sharing a tenth of their income and assets in this special way today.

## HOW AMERICA'S EARLY MILLIONAIRES MADE IT

Many of America's early millionaires used this prosperity method and pointed it out as the formula that brought them riches. The list includes the Colgate, Heinz, Kraft, and Rockefeller families. The illustrious and controversial John D.

Rockefeller made systematic tithing a lifelong habit, and *his practice of tithing preceded his accumulation of vast wealth.* *

It has often been reported that in 1855, he tithed ten percent from his total earnings of $95.00. The next year, his tithes grew from $9.50 to $28.37. The following year, they increased to $72.22. The next year, his tithes totaled $107.35. The following year, they had grown to $671.85. Five years later, his tithes had expanded to $5,489.62 for the year. They remained stationary for about a decade. Then, in 1878, they rose to $23,458.65 for the year. By 1881 his annual tithes had more than doubled. In 1884, his tithes had doubled again to $119,109.48. In 1887, his tithes exceeded a quarter of a million dollars, and in 1890, they topped the million-dollar mark!

John D. Rockefeller felt that making money and giving it away was a person's highest duty. He said, "A man should make all he can and give away all he can." *Between 1855 and 1934, he reportedly gave away $531 million.* One of the major secrets of his success was that he recognized God as the source of his supply and put God first financially. When people tried to criticize the Rockefeller wealth, he had a standard reply, "God gave me my money." He passed along this success secret to his family, and between 1917 and 1959, John D. Rockefeller Jr. reportedly gave away $474 million. The continuing philanthropy of the Rockefeller family has become legend.

Lest the success of the Rockefellers seem far-fetched in comparison to that of your own life, allow me to share the experiences of other workaday tithers.

---

* See the book by Myer Kutz, *Rockefeller Power, America's Chosen Family* (New York, N.Y.: Simon and Schuster, 1974).

## HOW SHE PAID OFF A $15,000 INDEBTEDNESS

When you first consider impersonally giving away one-tenth of your income, you may feel you cannot afford to do so because the universe has not yet richly endowed you in tangible ways. Yet you can be assured that you have been abundantly endowed in intangible ways with gifts of life, mind power, and talents that can begin to produce tangible results of increased abundance in your life. *The more you share with the universe, the more you will open your mind to receive, and the more you will be shown how to develop your talents and abilities, thus enriching your life.*

At a time when she was $15,000 in debt, a businesswoman heard that you can tithe your way out of indebtedness. She decided it was reasonable to believe that *when you withhold from God's treasury, you stop the flow of substance into your own treasury.* So in the face of financial difficulties, she began to tithe.

Two years later, she had paid off the $15,000 indebtedness and, for the first time, she had $7,000 in the bank. She celebrated by taking her first vacation in years. Later she said, "My fortunes changed when I began to put God first financially. *Faithful tithers always prosper.*"

## AN ACCOUNTANT'S FINANCIAL DISCOVERY

Accountants are regarded as very prudent people. Their job is to help clients conserve their income rather than dissipate it. But a Los Angeles public accountant recently said to me, "I have noticed that my clients who tithe, prosper. Their incomes continue to go up, up, up year after year. When I have a client who is having financial difficulties and not prospering, he is never a tither."

## WHY THEIR INCOME WAS $3,000 LESS

A musician with the Los Angeles Philharmonic Orchestra was a firm believer in tithing, but his wife handled their financial affairs. He had asked her to tithe a tenth of their gross income on a regular basis. Yet while preparing their income tax returns, their accountant made a discovery that startled the musician. Their income was $3,000 less than it had been the year before. Since both he and his wife had worked steadily that year, the musician could not understand this decrease.

In discussing the matter with his wife, he finally asked, "Did you tithe one-tenth of our entire income this year?"

"No, I did not," she admitted hesitantly. "When the children had all that dental work done, I decided we could not afford to tithe right then."

"How much did you withhold in tithes?" her husband inquired.

"Three hundred dollars," was the reply.

"That explains why our income was exactly $3,000 less this year," her husband commented.

His wife vowed never again to withhold any portion of their tithes.


## PROSPEROUS THINKING ISN'T ENOUGH

From two secretaries I once learned a valuable lesson. One was a student of prosperous thinking. Of these two employees, you would have thought she was the more successful and prosperous, wouldn't you? But she was not. She felt that mind power was sufficient to help her overcome all problems in life and make her successful, so she did not tithe. She didn't think it was necessary. Yet she did not get the raises in pay or promotions that the second secretary got. She kept wondering why.

The second secretary was a member of a traditional church that emphasized a "hellfire and damnation" teaching. Needless to say, she was a negative thinker. But she tithed, because her church required it.

Nevertheless, through the act of putting God first financially, she seemed to be lifted up into a spiritual realm above that of the law of cause and effect, so even her negative thinking did not keep her good from her. She and her husband were "well-fixed." Their assets included a spacious home, several cars, paid-up life insurance and annuities, rental properties, and a large savings account.

It was a shock to the first secretary to realize that prosperous thinking wasn't enough. Soon after she "wised up" and began to tithe, she was offered a far better job, which moved her out of that office and into more harmonious and prosperous surroundings. She proved that *for the person who boldly shares the tenth, life can become ten times easier.*

## THE PUBLIC'S FASCINATION
## WITH THIS PROSPERITY PRINCIPLE

I get more mail about the benefits of tithing than about any of the other prosperity principles I have written about during the past several decades. It has been a source of delight to me to learn how eager people are to know about the prospering power of tithing.

Unfortunately, the random offering method—spasmodic giving and sharing—has so often been emphasized, while the biblical method of giving through systematic tithing has often not been properly taught. There is nothing wrong with the random method of giving—as far as it goes. But it does not go far enough in helping a person to develop a stable prosperity consciousness. Spasmodic giving leads to spasmodic receiving. Random offerings were also given in biblical times, but over and above the regular tithes. "The tenth shall be holy unto Jehovah" was the rule. (Leviticus 27:32)

As pointed out in my book *The Millionaires of Genesis*, Jacob became a millionaire after he made a Success Covenant\* with God in which he pledged, "Of all that thou shalt give me I will surely give the tenth unto thee." (Genesis 28:22)

## TITHING GROSS OR NET

Strictly speaking, biblical tithing consisted of "a tenth of all." (Genesis 14:20) If you are not yet ready in your thinking to tithe from your gross income, you will want to consider tithing from your net income. But you will want to consider invoking ten, the magic number of increase, to some degree. Tithing is an act of faith that acts on the rich substance of the universe to prosper you mightily and to expand your world within and without in ways you would not have dreamed possible.

*Tithing releases a mystical power to prosper you.* Do not try to reason through the power of tithing. There is nothing reasonable about a miracle, and there is nothing reasonable about the miracle power of tithing. It is an act of faith that prospers. When you systematically tithe *first*, before paying bills or meeting financial obligations, you will find that the other ninety percent of your income goes much further. You will

---

\* For a free copy of the author's personalized Success Covenant, write her requesting it.

also be helped in many unforeseen ways. *Once you make a habit of giving, you will never miss those tithes. The very act of tithing will provide you with a sense of security, protection, and guidance that nothing else can.*

## HOW A BUSINESSMAN
## CAUSED HIS CHURCH TO PROSPER

At a time when there was never enough money to run a certain pioneer-style church in the hill country of Texas, one of the community's most prosperous citizens finally agreed to serve as church treasurer, but only on the condition that he would be allowed to handle the finances quietly, in his own way, for one year without having to explain his methods.

During that year, the little church thrived as never before. All the bills were paid, and there was an abundance of money left over at the end of the year. When the treasurer was asked to explain how he had performed this financial miracle he said, "It was simple. I am a businessman, and most of the church members are my customers. When a member of the church did business with me this year, I charged him ten percent extra. That was his tithe, which I passed on to the church. This ministry has prospered as never before this year from the tithes of its members—who didn't know they were tithing, *yet never missed it.*"

## WHERE YOU GIVE
## IS IMPORTANT TO YOUR SUCCESS

*Where* you give is important to your success. It is wise to give at the point or points where you are receiving spiritual help and inspiration—whether it be a church or a minister, teacher, practitioner, or spiritual counselor. Your tithes will enrich the recipient, so the organization or individual is freed from financial strain. This enables them to fulfill their high mission of uplifting humanity, unhindered by material cares, which can be so burdensome.

Perhaps this was why Jehovah instructed Moses that the priestly tribe of Israel was to receive *none* of the Promised Land. (Joshua 13:33; Numbers 18:21-24; Deuteronomy 14:27) *The priests of Israel became millionaires through the tithes bestowed upon them by the other eleven tribes, as proclaimed by Mosaic Law.* In turn, they shared "a tithe of the tithes" known as a "heave offering" with the place of worship. (Numbers 18:26-29) In this way, both the priests and the places of worship were provided for abundantly.

In turn, their freedom from material care helped them, as the spiritual leaders of Israel, to develop and generate a prosperity consciousness that was to bless those whom they served for many centuries to come. A group prosperity consciousness was developed during that era of Hebrew history that has persisted even into modern times. Someone has said, "A Jew can make more accidentally than a Gentile can make on purpose." It all began centuries ago with their prosperous habit of tithing.

## WHAT ABOUT CHARITY GIVING?

Is giving to charity or community events the same as tithing? No, not strictly speaking. For enlightened and spiritually evolving individuals, the highest form of philanthropy is that of giving to spiritually enlightened causes and individuals. The Hebrews of the Old Testament became wealthy when they gave the *first* tithe impersonally to their priests and places of worship. (Leviticus 27:20-33; Numbers 18:21-24; Deuteronomy 14:22-27) Their *second* tithe was a festival tithe. (Deuteronomy 12:6, 7) Their *third* tithe was a charity tithe. (Deuteronomy 14:28-29) They also shared of "the first fruits" of their crops, and made many other offerings. In addition, tithing was a required temple practice during Jesus' era and that of the early Christians.

If you are giving more than one-tenth, then you should feel freer to share your second or third tenth with charity or other humanitarian causes. But usually the first tenth should go to spiritual work or to workers whose philosophy is uplifting and helping humanity, and is one you agree with.

Of course, for individuals who have no spiritual inclinations or interest, giving to various charitable, cultural, educational, or humanitarian causes is most commendable and a great step forward in the development of their prosperity consciousness, as well as being beneficial to their soul growth. The recipient of their gifts is likewise assisted and benefited. However, according to the ancient laws of tithing, this is a secondary form of giving rather than the highest.

## PRAY ABOUT YOUR GIVING

It is important to pray about your giving. Ask a loving God to reveal to you *where* to share your tithes, and you will be guided in your giving, so all involved in your gift—both you as the giver and the receiver—will be prospered, uplifted, and blessed. As you evolve, grow, and change, so may your tithing practices—thus opening the door for you to receive in ever-increasing ways!

## SCATTERED TITHES CAN BRING
## SCATTERED RESULTS

One of the sins of many tithers is that they tend to scatter their tithes, giving to many causes. Scattered tithes tend to bring scattered, ineffectual results, both for the giver and for the recipient of those tithes. Since many good causes tend to suffer financially, your generous, concentrated tithes can be "manna from heaven" that assures financial stability for a single—or a relative few—worthy causes. Scattered giving to many causes does little to help any of them. Never be afraid of giving big tithes to one or two causes, if you wish to reap big results in your own life. Do not be afraid of giving "too much" for the benefit of the recipient of your gifts, either. That's rarely ever a danger! (And it is a limiting thought for all concerned.)

## THE PROSPERING POWER
## OF SECRECY AND RELEASE

Almost in anger a businessman said, "Why haven't I prospered? I tithed almost fifty percent of my income last year. Now I am broke, and none of the churches I shared my tithes with are willing to help me." Without meaning to, this man had probably violated two prosperity laws: secrecy and release.

The words "sacred" and "secret" have the same root meaning. Our giving is sacred and therefore should be kept secret. It is wise to give quietly with no strings attached, regardless of the amounts involved, not referring to them again. If large tithes are involved, it is often necessary to emotionally release and re-release them until one has a sense of freedom from them. There should be no sense of possessiveness about the tithes one shares anyway, regardless of their size, since all that we receive comes from God and is not ours to permanently own. In tithe-giving, we are only returning *to* God a portion of all that has already been given to us *by* God.

Also, it is usually wiser to give the tenth systematically and freely than to give much larger amounts spasmodically without releasing them. Tithing is not a "get-rich-quick" scheme by which you can force your good. "There is no rush in spirit." Instead, the act of tithing is a process of growth by which one evolves into larger giving (and larger receiving).

If one resents one's giving, then the practice of release is in order. To give and then make demands upon the recipient of one's gifts amounts to a bribe, not a tithe. The conscientious tither does not give for "show" or for publicity. The recipient of one's tithes should be equally as quiet about such gifts. Otherwise it is easy to dissipate and "talk away one's good." As the ancient people knew, there is prospering power in secrecy and in release.

## A CLOSING PROMISE OF VAST BENEFITS

The word "prosper" in its root means "wholeness." That is what the prophet Malachi promised in the last book of the Old Testament to those who tithe. He pointed out that *tithing can prove to be the best investment in successful living you can make over the years, and also the most soul-satisfying.*

Although there are many biblical promises made to the tither, perhaps the ones best describing its vast benefits are those he pointed out in Malachi 3:7-12.

*First,* he described the cause of the non-tither's problems:

From the days of your father ye have turned aside from mine ordinances, and have not kept them. Return unto me, and I will return unto you, said Jehovah of Hosts. But ye say, Wherein shall we return? Will a man rob God? Yet ye rob me. But ye say, Wherein have we robbed thee? In tithes and offerings. Ye are cursed with the curse; for ye rob me, even this whole nation.

***Second****, he described the lavish blessings due the tither:*

Bring ye the whole tithe into the storehouse, that there may be food in my house, and prove me now herewith, said Jehovah of Hosts, if I will not open you the windows of heaven, and pour you out a blessing, that there shall not be room enough to receive it.

***Third****, he promised divine protection to the tither:*

And I will rebuke the devourer for your sakes, and he shall not destroy the fruits of your ground; neither shall your vine cast its fruit before the time in the field, saith Jehovah of Hosts.

***Fourth****, he promised personal happiness and universal prestige to the tither:*

And all the nations shall call you happy; for ye shall be a delightsome land, said Jehovah of Hosts.

# YOUR GIFT OF AGREEMENT

## — Chapter 8 —

Now that you have learned how to open your mind to receive, can you actually do it? Here's one way to begin.

In ancient times there was a secret teaching, which to many people is still a secret today. It was based on a strong success principle: the *power of agreement*. This teaching declares that you came into this world equipped to meet every demand that this world will make upon you, but that you must be willing to cooperate with situations, people, and events. When you cooperate with life in these ways, then life cooperates with you.

And how do you cooperate with life—especially when you encounter difficult people, difficult situations, or difficult events?

That ancient teaching gives this answer: "When you agree with life, then life agrees with you. Always there is ground for agreement. Agree, and withdraw in peace."

## THE AUTHOR'S DISCOVERY

I never fully realized the power of agreement with other people until I was married to my late husband, Dr. Ponder. We seemed to agree on just about everything—certainly on issues of importance. The result was that, together, we were able to experience what seemed to us like miracles during our brief marriage, before his early passing. Everything came so much easier when he and I agreed with each other, when we worked together to bring to pass that which we had agreed upon.

Years later, in another marriage, I had the same experience. My husband even retired from his practice to help with my work. We talked everything over, agreed on our goals, then went our separate ways each day to do our individual tasks. Over a long period of time, we too experienced results that seemed miraculous to us—without undue effort or strain. Only agreement.

## THE POWER OF DISAGREEMENT

Most people know about the power of *disagreement*. Those who are habitually disagreeable, who tend to battle their way through life, are more likely to suffer from ill health or from emotional or financial problems, which are often caused by their fighting attitudes.

"What you fight to get, you fight to keep" is an age-old axiom. How to solve this problem? If you agree where you can agree, and refrain from dwelling on the points about which you cannot agree, you remain in harmony with the universe and with each other. *Always there is ground for agreement, so agree—and withdraw in peace.*

## THE AUTHOR'S RECENT EXPERIENCE

While I was writing this chapter, I had occasion to prove its theory:

I was forced to cooperate outwardly with people, situations, and events with which I did not inwardly agree. But I realized that lack of cooperation would bring inharmony, friction, and resistance, which could cause unnecessary problems. The solution was to agree where I could agree, and withdraw in peace.

The parties and situations involved were so relieved that I did not act resistant, but cooperated instead. The happy result was that they gradually began to cooperate with me, so no unnecessary problems or inharmonies developed. By my agreeing and withdrawing in peace, they began to cooperate, and friction was avoided. Problems were solved and peace was restored. That experience reinforced this Truth: when we cooperate with life, life then cooperates with us.

## FROM UNHAPPINESS TO DESIRED GOALS

I once had a middle-aged friend, a widow, who was extremely attractive. She was quite successful in business and had many admiring friends. Her children from a previous marriage were grown, and she felt she had come to a time of life when she should be thriving.

But she was constantly unhappy. Rather than appreciating the blessings she had, she dwelled constantly on her desire to remarry. I suggested that she get quiet and practice the principle of agreement with circumstances. Specifically, I suggested that she agree with everything that had already come to her and not "talk her good away"—that she accept the blessings she enjoyed, not fuss about what she didn't have—and get in harmony with the universe so greater good could come to her at an appropriate time.

Finally she met a man who seemed to be wonderful, and they became engaged. She was ecstatic and began making wedding plans, but suddenly "Mr. Wonderful" changed his mind and left town. She became so distraught that she made herself physically ill. I found myself visiting her in the hospital, where in a highly agitated state of mind, she refused to be consoled.

I reminded her that we are never in charge of what others will do, and suggested that she again declare her agreement with her circumstances, past and present, and have confidence that everything would work out.

After a while she resumed her normal life, and I suggested she mentally declare that the next step in the Divine Plan of her life was now appearing. She followed my suggestion, and sympathetic friends soon invited her back to her home town, where they entertained her at their country club. There she met a businessman who immediately fell in love with her. They soon married and spent a number of years together. Then he passed on, leaving her a major inheritance.

She contacted me again, and said, "As much as I loved my late husband, I do not care to spend the last part of my life alone, even if I am wealthy." I reminded her about the principle of agreement and suggested that she set her goal in consciousness—and keep quiet about it.

Rather quickly she met her future husband. The last I heard, both were experiencing the joys of marital bliss together in their senior years.

But nothing had worked out until this lady learned the power of agreement. Then everything happened for the best, and she grew into her expanded good—which continued to expand.

## A LESSON LEARNED

Most people are familiar with the biblical admonition "Agree with thine adversary quickly." (Matt. 5:25) A husband once practiced this kind of agreement when, at the end of his first year of marriage, his wife decided the time had come to tell him all about his faults.

She said, "Now that we have been married a year, we should be able to *be honest* with each other. So I am going to point out all your faults to you, dear. Afterward, you can point out all my faults to me."

She then proceeded with a long list of woes. When she finished, she said, "Now it's your turn. Tell me all that is wrong with me."

Her very wise husband said, "My dear, you are perfect in every way. I would not have one thing about you changed."

There was a long silence—after which this wife inwardly vowed she would never again dwell upon her husband's faults. She would focus only on the good points. That decision contributed greatly to their having a long, happy, enduring marriage.

## THE POWER OF BIBLICAL AGREEMENT

The Bible is clear in its teachings on the power of agreement. In the Old Testament, Amos asked, "Shall two walk together, except they have agreed?" (Amos 3:3) The New Testament, in addition to Jesus' well-known counsel "Agree with thine adversary quickly" (Matt. 5:25), relates that the Apostle Paul also emphasized it! "And all that believed were together, and had all things common." (Acts 2:44) Later, in his epistle to the Romans, Paul wrote of the power of their being "of one accord." (Romans 15:6) Paul and Timothy wrote in their epistle to the Philippians of the power of being "of one accord, of one mind." (Phil. 2:2) Some historians feel that the growth of the early Christians throughout the ancient world was in part because they were taught and they practiced this power of agreement.

## NO IMPOSSIBLE SITUATION

Another version of the power of agreement can be found in a present-day success formula: "Two agreed tune in on a Third Power." This aligns with Jesus' oft-quoted promise: "If two of you shall agree on earth as touching anything that they shall ask, it shall be done for them of my Father." (Matt. 18:19)

This even applies to apparently impossible situations. When a wealthy widow told me she was praying to meet a man she might marry and asked me to join her in that prayer, I felt her faith was greater than mine about the matter. Nevertheless I prayed with her.

This lady was blessed with a nice home, a comfortable lifetime income, and several well-to-do, married daughters. However she gave little attention to her personal appearance, seeming almost to prefer looking dowdy, and her disposition was not always pleasant, since she felt her wealth would lead people to overlook everything else about her.

Shortly after we prayed for a husband for her, one of the wealthiest men in our town was visited by his brother, who was equally wealthy, and whose wife had recently died. The local brother decided that since these two people—his out-of-town brother and the widow—were now both alone and of equal status financially, they should meet. When they did, the visiting brother was immediately attracted to this lady and soon asked her to marry him.

This time she returned to see me—in a panic.

"What shall I do? I don't want to leave my comfortable home and my much-loved daughters who live nearby, and then go to some faraway place to live among strangers."

Eventually she declined her suitor's offer of marriage. The power of agreement between us had worked for her, but ultimately to no avail, because she really didn't want what she and I had prayed for!

## FROM POVERTY TO AFFLUENCE

Where prosperity is concerned, the power of agreement is not affected by bank accounts or financial assets, and it works as well for the everyday people as it does for the affluent.

My mother used to take my brother, sister, and me to visit a wealthy aunt and uncle of hers. The aunt and uncle lived in an old, Southern-style, columned mansion, and we always looked forward to those visits as a great treat.

Mother was very proud of the fact that when this couple married, they had done so without parental consent (since each family felt the other was too poor to marry into). But love won out over economics.

Once they were married, they began to spend at least an hour each morning talking business. That was an era when women were not supposed to bother with business or even have opinions about it. Nevertheless, my mother's aunt did have opinions *and* her husband listened to her. They were in the cotton business, and she talked to her husband about cotton futures, which were considered a risky but lucrative investment down South. Nevertheless, her husband listened to her. They would discuss past investments and agree on the best way to proceed for success.

They continued these daily morning meetings for years, always talking about various aspects of their business as it grew. In due time they had "agreed their way" into a comfortable income and later into becoming the wealthiest couple in their town. It was during this era that my mother proudly took us to visit them.

That was my first introduction to an affluent atmosphere, and having it in our family was nice. But perhaps more important to me was learning *how* they had acquired their wealth— for the method they had used so successfully was *agreement*.

## HOW IMMIGRANTS SUCCEEDED

Here is a slightly different approach that worked for an immigrant couple:

They were born in Europe but, upon their engagement, decided they wanted to live, work, and raise a family in America. So they agreed that the fiancé would come to this country first and get settled in a job, after which he would send for his betrothed. Then they would be married and proceed with their plans. The woman waited for quite a while before her fiancé felt the time was right for her to join him—but that time finally arrived.

After they married, they decided that each morning they would spend an hour studying inspirational literature, reading their Bible, and planning out their day, then proceed accordingly. Their early-morning study and agreement method worked so well that they soon had developed their own business, which grew and grew. When I later met them, they had their own factory, a home in the most affluent part of town, and a very pleasant way of life.

## DECLARE IT GOOD

Another phase of the power of agreement is to agree with the good in an adverse situation even when it's in the past. When you are no longer disturbed by its existence—in fact or in your memories—it then can finally leave your life, often quickly. When you agree with a situation by pronouncing it good—whether it seems to be good or not—you are agreeing with the *unseen* good in the situation. You are opening the way for it to appear.

There once was a divorced man who'd had several unhappy marriages. In conversations with a therapist, he was advised to go back in his thinking to his first marriage and find some point of agreement with his wife in that marriage, then release the marriage, forgive his ex-partner, and mentally declare that the marriage had been a success.

When this man consciously thought about that marriage, he realized how much he still resented his first wife. He also realized that he had carried resentment into later relationships and, without realizing it, unconsciously directed that resentment toward his later wives. So none of his marriages had worked out.

For that first (and each succeeding) relationship, he now said mentally to the former wife: "I FORGIVE YOU. I RELEASE YOU. OUR MARRIAGE WAS FOR GOOD. OUR RELATIONSHIP WAS SUCCESSFUL BECAUSE WE BOTH LEARNED FROM IT." Later, when he married again, it proved to be a happy union because he mentally declared it a success from the start. He constantly looked for and emphasized the points of agreement.

## NO EXPERIENCE IS A FAILURE

All of us should stop saying we have "failed in marriage" or have "failed in business" or are in "failing health." We have never failed in any experience. Why? Because we *learned* from it. So long as we keep our thoughts on personal troubles and can't get beyond regarding them *as* "troubles," we bind them to us. But when we look upward in agreement toward answers and solutions, the very forces of heaven rush to our aid.

To do this, a businessman once developed his own successful method for using the power of agreement. He said, "I call every event in my life by the same name: *success*! If I have a failure, I call it a success, and it always proves to be a success in some way. I agree with the good in every experience, and the good agrees with me."

A widow used the power of agreement in a different way. At the time of her bereavement, a former friend was very rude to her. The rudeness seemed especially cruel, coming at that sensitive time.

Nevertheless, the widow said to herself, "I will only remember that this woman has been very kind to me in the past. There are many good things I can remember about her, so it does not matter what she says or does now." As the widow held to this line of reasoning, the former friend—who had no idea the woman was maintaining this positive attitude— responded by finding a good job for her.

The lesson here? When, through using the principle of agreement, we reverse our thinking about people, they often reverse their behavior toward us!

## AGREE WITH THE GOOD ANYWAY

What of the usual trouble you meet in the office or at home? When that kind of apparently negative situation shows up, the power of agreement takes us right over it. For example, you can respond to trouble by saying, "I do not accept that," which really means, "I refuse to get upset about it." When you do not give it any mental or emotional power, it cannot affect you. Furthermore, it cannot last. The only way a negative condition can continue to hurt you is for you to continue to feel bad about it. *You don't get hurt by the things you refuse to feel bad about.*

This doesn't mean not to do what you can to correct matters, and you can always start doing so by giving them the right thought. Then—stop talking about them or noticing them. Release them. (Most people undo their good with needless talk.) When you can no longer be disturbed by a negative situation, it will hold no power over you, and it can fade from your experience. You can "agree" it right out of your life!

## A DECADE OF AGREEMENT WORKS

A young couple, very much in love, planned to marry—only to discover that the future bride had what was considered an incurable health problem. However, both were believers in the power of prayer as a part of the healing process, so her fiancé told her he would wait while they worked toward her complete wholeness. They agreed their marriage was worth waiting for.

For ten years—an entire decade—this betrothed couple remained in agreement with their goal of a complete recovery and a subsequent happy marriage. They believed in that well-known adage, "Two agreed tune in on a Third Power."

In that ten-year period, along with the prescribed medical treatment, they studied inspirational books and Bible promises, and practiced inspirational thinking, as they affirmed "wholeness and health." The results were that the bride-to-be experienced a gradual health recovery.

After a beautiful wedding, they thankfully enjoyed a satisfying marriage for many years together, proving the success
power of "two agreed" against all odds.

## GROUP AGREEMENT CAN CLEAR OUT FRICTION

A minister was once faced with a vocal minority of critics
in his church. His private prayer group agreed to pray with him
that "everything and everybody that does not support the divine plan for this ministry is released to find their good elsewhere." No defense by the minister, or of him, was made to the
critics. They were treated with the same appreciation and re-
spect as the rest of the congregation.

Nevertheless, the critics gradually disappeared from the
church. One Sunday one of the ushers asked, "Where is everybody? What's happened? Some people are no longer attending
who once did." A member of the Prayer Ministry said, "It's
simple. We 'prayed them out.'"

The usher said, "I have heard of 'praying people into a
church,' but I've never heard of 'praying them out.'" The
member of the Prayer Ministry then explained that those who
had left were not in agreement with the minister or the church,
and though they were in the minority, their vocal criticism had
caused unnecessary inharmony and friction. That person also
reminded the usher that by releasing those who were not in
agreement and had left, those who remained had formed a vacuum for new, appreciative attendees to fill. The usher had
heard the vacuum theory but had never thought of its being applied in that way.

Within six weeks of the time the vocal critics were gone,
new, enthusiastic, prominent members of the community began
to appear and declare, "Where have you been? I've been looking for a church with this philosophy." They quickly became

members, volunteer workers, and tithers, and consistently brought in other new, appreciative attendees.

The result was that soon the church's attendance had doubled and so had its income. Plus, it was filled with a congregation of happy people who were eager to learn more of that church's teachings.

The power of agreement had done its perfect work.

## HOW IT WORKS FOR THOSE WHO ARE ALONE

Perhaps you're thinking, "But I am alone right now. I have no one to join me in using the agreement method. How can I get results?" Do not let this worry you, for the power of agreement is so strong that it works whether your agreement is made with the knowledge of another person or simply spoken in your own heart.

A woman in business found herself constantly in the presence of a man who always talked lack, poverty, and limitation. This made her feel impoverished, and her finances suffered.

She knew that in order to demonstrate supply she must feel prosperous again, yet she heard herself constantly blaming this man for her dwindling business. Then she remembered the power of agreement. At that point she reversed her thinking. Seeing past his negative personality and agreeing instead with the well-being she was certain would soon be forthcoming, she said to herself, "This man is in my life for my good and for my prosperity."

Soon, through this very man, she met a woman for whom she performed a business service and received several thousand dollars. Furthermore, the man in question moved to a distant city and faded out of her life completely. But it all happened only after she had quietly—alone—agreed with the good in the situation. She never again underestimated the ability of her own private power of agreement to bring favorable results.

## HEALING POWER

The power in agreement can also be used by one person for healing. A woman worked diligently to heal her husband through affirmative prayer. But every time she tried it, her husband got worse. Finally a friend said to her, "Without realizing it, you may be trying mentally to *will* your husband back to health. You may be trying to force him mentally to accept what you think is best for him, and he is subconsciously fighting back. The soul of every person always wants freedom to choose. Release him, leave him alone. Tell him mentally that he can get just as sick as he likes, that he can remain sick as long as he wishes, that you have released him to do whatever he wants to do. Tell him he is a free soul."

This wife followed this advice. Later she said, "I have never seen a person get well so fast as my husband did."

## AGREEMENT MEDITATION

I CAME INTO THIS LIFE EQUIPPED TO MEET EVERY DEMAND THE WORLD MAKES UPON ME. BUT I MUST BE WILLING TO COOPERATE WITH LIFE, SO LIFE CAN COOPERATE WITH ME.

I DECLARE EVERY SITUATION IN MY LIFE A SUCCESS. I HAVE NEVER FAILED IN ANY EXPERIENCE, BECAUSE I LEARNED FROM IT.

ALWAYS THERE IS ROOM FOR AGREEMENT. I GRANT ITS PRESENCE BY AGREEING WITH THE GOOD. THEN I WITHDRAW IN PEACE.

# THAT GOLDEN SUNBURST

My readers have sometimes asked the meaning of the golden sunburst on the covers of my books. One commented, "When I see that gold symbol in a bookstore, I know a Ponder book is involved, and I always take a look at it." Another reader said that's how she *finds* my books—by looking for that sunburst.

The symbol was not an original idea with me. It came from one of my publishers, the late Arthur Peattie of DeVorss & Co., who suggested that we use it on all my books for its beauty and as a symbol of distinction. His suggestion proved to be a popular one.

Here is its meaning, which ties in perfectly with the Wholeness I write about in all of my books: *In ancient times people of note often bore "seals" on their possessions as indications of their success and prominence. The golden sunburst found on the Ponder books is such a seal—one of enlightenment and abundance. Its fifteen points symbolize the breaking up of hard conditions and the expansion that enlightenment can bring—into one's royal heritage of increased health, wealth, and happiness.*

See

*AN IMPORTANT NOTE FROM THE AUTHOR*
on the next page.

# AN IMPORTANT NOTE FROM THE AUTHOR

Through the generous outpouring of their tithes over the years, readers of my books have helped me financially to establish three new churches—the most recent being a global ministry, the nondenominational *Unity Church Worldwide*, with headquarters in Palm Desert, California. Many thanks for your help in the past and for all you continue to share.

You are also invited to share your tithes with the churches of your choice—especially those that teach the truths stressed in this book. Such churches include the nondenominational churches of Unity, Centers for Spiritual Living, Religious Science (Science of Mind), Divine Science, and others that are related, many of which are part of the International New Thought Movement. (For a list of these churches, write The International New Thought Alliance, 5003 E. Broadway Road, Mesa, AZ 85206 USA.) Your support of churches such as these can help spread the prosperous Truth that humanity is now seeking in this oncoming age of enlightenment.

---

Readers who would like to contact Catherine Ponder or her *Unity Church Worldwide* ministry for prayer help, literature, or other reasons may reach her at PO Box 4640, Palm Springs, CA 92263 USA.